A CELEBRATION
OF ART &
ARCHITECTURE

© Colin Amery and National Gallery
Publications Limited 1991

All rights reserved. No part of this publication
may be transmitted in any form or by any
means, electronic or mechanical, including
photocopy, recording, or any information
storage and retrieval system, without the prior
permission in writing from the publisher.

First published in Great Britain in 1991 by
National Gallery Publications Limited
5/6 Pall Mall East, London SW1Y 5BA

Library of Congress Catalog Card Number:
91-61062

British Library Cataloguing in Publication Data
Amery, Colin, 1944–
A celebration of art and architecture: the
National Gallery Sainsbury Wing.
1. Art galleries: Architecture
I. Title
727.70942132

ISBN 0-947645-87-X *paperback*
      0-947645-86-1 *hardback*

Designed and Art Directed by Peter Baistow
Editors: Felicity Luard and Luci Collings
Commissioned photography by Phil Starling
Foldout drawing by Paul Draper
Printed in Great Britain by
Balding + Mansell plc, London and Wisbech

Front cover: The Sainsbury Wing.
Back cover: The central galleries looking
towards Raphael's *Crucified Christ c.* 1503.

A CELEBRATION OF ART & ARCHITECTURE

COLIN AMERY

NATIONAL
GALLERY
LONDON

CONTENTS

he foldout drawing on pages 7–10 shows in cut-away form the unfolding of the processional progression of great galleries old and new, with details of the exterior on the left and details of the interior on the right. The architecture of the Sainsbury Wing is carefully composed of classical elements – some taken from William Wilkins's Gallery and some transformed from Italian Renaissance architecture – adapted to make an imposing and intricate new London landmark.
Page 5 *Sassetta,* The Dream of the Young Saint Francis, *completed 1444.*
Page 6 *Carlo Crivelli,* The Annunciation, with Saint Emidius *(detail), 1486.*
Page 11 *Antonello da Messina,* Saint Jerome in his Study *(detail),* c. *1475–6.*
Page 12 *Hans Memlinc,* The Virgin and Child with Saints and Donors *(detail),* c. *1475.*

ELLINI·LEONARDO·RAPHAEL

Buildings over the years have, I think, suffered many worse insults than to be called a 'carbuncle'. Few buildings have aroused as much public feeling, however, as that intended for the Hampton site next to the National Gallery. The history of the competition for an extension is carefully related by Colin Amery in this book – and architects will once again be able to debate the justice of the public's views on the matter!

I am certainly not averse to partnerships between culture and commerce, but it is clear that the original competition was asking far too much in requiring a building which effectively served *three* masters, which provided appropriate housing for one of the finest art collections in the world, which had to face on to one of the finest – certainly the *liveliest* – of urban spaces in London, *and* at the same time provide rentable space. The Sainsburys are much to be thanked for sorting out this tangle by acting as patrons, and putting commerce in a more appropriate place.

The debate will now rage, I'm sure, about how good a building Mr Venturi has given us. I will leave that to others to decide – though I *will* say that I think the interiors very promising as spaces in which to reflect upon art.

This book is the last act in a drama that I'm sure everyone concerned – and that means most of us! – have learnt from. It is also the first symbol of a new age for the National Gallery. I hope the building serves the Gallery and its growing public as well as it can.

FOREWORD   Lord Rothschild

After 50 years, thanks to great and imaginative generosity, the saga of the Hampton site has come to an end, and indeed a very happy one, meeting the needs of the National Gallery, and adding, we believe, a distinguished building of great quality to London.

More often than not museum buildings give rise to sharp differences in matters of approach and style. Some 150 years ago 'our much loved and elegant friend', as HRH The Prince of Wales described William Wilkins's National Gallery building, was highly controversial and much disliked. Pugin and Brittan's 1839 edition of *Illustrations of the Public Buildings of London* commented: 'Not one of our lately erected buildings has been the object of more general and unqualified censure.' The problems of the Hampton site have been every bit as fraught as those of the original National Gallery building, but in addition to questions of taste and style the Trustees of the National Gallery have had to contend with the factor of there being no public money available for the construction of a new building. In the nineteenth century, while it was customary for benefactors to donate paintings to the National Gallery, the idea of paying for the building itself would hardly have crossed their minds. Those costs would have been perceived as the responsibility of Government, albeit that even over the Wilkins building they were the subject of much agony and debate.

As we approach the end of the twentieth century, the notion of public museum buildings being a luxury the nation could ill afford to pay for has unhappily become more and more accepted by successive British Governments and private enterprise has been encouraged to help out. Not surprisingly the response has been limited, although the Sainsbury Centre for the Visual Arts in East Anglia and the Clore Gallery at the Tate provide splendid examples of privately funded museums. The Trustees of the National Gallery had always hoped that any building on the Hampton site would be for its sole use, but it seemed beyond the realms of possibility that a donor would ever emerge to make this possible. Government had to its credit provided the necessary funds in 1958 for the acquisition of the site, specifically for an extension. More than 20 years went by until, in 1981, the Trustees decided, albeit with a degree of reluctance and considerable misgivings, to put forward a scheme to the Government for a new extension where the costs of the gallery space on the top floor would be met by the 'planning gain' arising from the value of commercial office space to be built by a developer on the other floors. Government's contribution would be to grant a long lease of the site to the developer for a peppercorn rent. In December 1981 the Hampton site competition was announced at a press conference by Mr Michael Heseltine, who was then as now Secretary of State for the Environment.

It was the acceptance of this compromise that led to the *annus terribilis* of 1984. None of the architectural schemes put forward received wide support or enthusiasm and a number of critics gave full voice to their feelings in their evidence before the public inquiry. in April, Stephen Gardiner began his evidence by saying:

> I think it is a national disgrace that it is proposed that the treasures of the National Gallery – the finest collection of Renaissance paintings in the world – should be put on the top of an office block . . . imagine the Crown Jewels being exhibited on the top of a Marks and Spencer building. What would the public response be to that, I wonder?

In May the Prince of Wales delivered the *coup de grâce* when he described the chosen design as a 'monstrous carbuncle'. Nemesis finally came in September when the Secretary of State for the Environment, Mr Patrick Jenkin, refused planning permission for the project on the grounds that it constituted 'an unwelcome intrusion . . . altogether inappropriate for this site of national importance'. A few days later Christopher Booker in a letter to *The Times* wrote:

> There might now seem to be an overwhelming case for launching a public appeal simply to construct a proper purpose-built extension to the gallery . . . and the building's design would be no longer bedevilled by the ambivalent considerations of public need and private gain which have in large part led to the present impasse.

The chances of a public appeal succeeding seemed very remote, although the Trustees continued to hope that some great act of imaginative sponsorship might extricate them from the difficult situation that confronted them. My predecessor, Lord Annan, and the Director, Sir Michael Levey, whose doubts had become more and more acute over the months, somehow maintained their resolve, and the battered Trustees, some of whom had from the beginning shared the view expressed by the Prince, decided to make one more effort to find the necessary financial support for a building to be used exclusively by the National Gallery. Exploratory discussions were held with one or two individuals but the costs of the project were increasingly daunting. Towards the very end of the year quite unexpectedly and at his own initiative Sir John Sainsbury, now Lord Sainsbury, who had served as a Trustee of the National Gallery from 1976 to 1983, contacted the Trustees to put forward his and his family's astonishingly generous idea of a gift to the nation of the entire extension building. Overwhelmed, we made every possible effort to overcome the daunting problems and the many hurdles that remained. From December 1984 until April 1985, John and his brothers, Simon and Timothy, worked closely with Lord Annan, Caryl Hubbard – who as a Trustee has devoted herself for more than six years to the creation of the building, Michael Levey and myself. It would be a *sine qua non* that the Government would agree to pay for the future maintenance of the new building. The disappointed developers, Trafalgar House, had to be persuaded to give up their lease of the site and their compensation settled. There was then the question of how to carry out the development which we wanted to undertake on our own with the Sainsbury family and without the involvement of the Government through the Property Services Agency.

We decided on a unique form of cooperation through the vehicle of The Hampton Site Company, which we formed with a board consisting of the donors and the Trustees. In continental Europe new museum buildings are funded and built by central or local government, while in the United States of America new projects are carried out by the management of the museum, with help from a donor being limited in the main to finance. Ours was to be a close working relationship with the Sainsbury family, who have made available to us their exceptional administrative and business skills, in addition to meeting the costs of the building. Since the project began there have been more than 50 meetings of the full Hampton Site Company Board, while the steering committee of the Board under the perfectionist chairmanship of Simon Sainsbury has been in virtually continuous session.

1985 was the *annus mirabilis* of the National Gallery: on 2 April came the formal announcement of the Sainsbury family's gift of the building. Good fortune of this kind was without parallel in the history of the National Gallery, but it was to be followed shortly afterwards by Mr J. Paul Getty Jr's gift of an endowment fund, the largest single donation ever given to an institution in this country. We decided to form a selection committee to choose the architect for the building, with membership made up of the three Sainsbury brothers, Sir Michael Levey, Allan Braham and Michael Wilson from the

National Gallery, and from the Trustees, Lord Annan, until his retirement in June 1985, Lord Dufferin, Caryl Hubbard, Bridget Riley, Stuart Young and myself. In addition we invited Sir Isaiah Berlin, as a former Trustee whose advice we rightly felt would be invaluable, and Stuart Lipton, together with his colleague Vincent Wang, who have given us the benefit of their immense knowledge and experience in the planning and construction of buildings. As expert advisers we invited Ada Louise Huxtable, the distinguished former architectural correspondent of the *New York Times*, as a guide to the architects of America, and Colin Amery, her English counterpart and architectural correspondent of the *Financial Times*, to help us in our choice of architect in Britain and continental Europe. Colin Amery in his admirable and most informative book describes in detail the intensive selection process which continued for some nine months and which ended with the unanimous choice of Robert Venturi of Venturi, Rauch and Scott Brown of Philadelphia.

Now more than five years later the building has been completed, the useful life of the Hampton Site Company is over and we ask ourselves why this site and building have assumed such importance, not just in London or indeed in England but also for those who care about the arts in the rest of the world. The site on which the Sainsbury Wing now stands is after all not a very large one, and the National Gallery's Collection amounts to about 2,200 paintings in total, less than a third of the Royal Collection. In the new building fewer than 250 Early Renaissance works are displayed. The whole building, including the entrance hall, temporary exhibition space, theatre, restaurant, conference rooms and the top floor galleries, amounts to 90,000 square feet. By contrast, the new Richelieu Wing development at the Louvre, which will be opened in 1993, is about three times as large. An even more spectacular perspective could be drawn with the Smithsonian Institute in Washington, whose collection amounts to no less than 137 million objects, with new acquisitions forecast at the rate of 700,000 per year.

In the context of London, there were understandable reasons for people minding so much about the future of the site. Although only occupying the northwest corner of Trafalgar Square, it lies on the ceremonial route. Jubilee Walk connects Leicester Square to Trafalgar Square, but the two squares have always remained strangely disconnected and poles apart. The urban thoroughfare in its new form, we hope, will change this. More generally, we have belatedly become more aware of the wounds inflicted on London in the post-war period by inferior, and sometimes very inferior, architecture. We sensed therefore the opportunity of putting up a museum building of quality which could become a centre for the cultural life of our capital city and the nation. The impact of the few distinguished new museums that had been built – the Burrell Collection in Glasgow, the Sainsbury Centre in East Anglia and the Clore extension at the Tate – could still hardly be compared with the East Wing of the National Gallery of Washington, or with the new buildings at the Louvre in Paris. We live at a time when the museum building rather than the cathedral, church or railway station has become the architect's paramount vehicle of expression in the West, and the public have become passionately interested in the architectural debate. Was the building of the Pyramid in the forecourt of the Louvre, the most spectacular invasion of an historic centre by a modern building, appropriate or inappropriate? Should a truly modern building have been put up in Trafalgar Square? Or, given the Wilkins building, its Greek classical neighbour, should another neo-classical beaux-arts type of building be designed, or some pastiche, or a post-modernist building attempting to be in sympathy both with the old and the new? Or would that symbolically represent a defeat of the modern movement, thereby putting the clock back by more than a decade? Could a modern architect create perfect gallery space for old master paintings? These were some of the questions that donors, Trustees and the National Gallery had to consider in their choice of an architect, remembering always that the interior architecture of the building was at least as important as the exterior. In the last analysis we all felt that everything should defer to the paintings.

Even the design of the space inside a museum has captured the public's imagination and interest. Expectations for the interior of a museum are now very different to what they were in the nineteenth century, when space was almost exclusively devoted to creating an atmosphere in which the serene contemplation of works of art was possible. As Venturi has pointed out, now only about one-third of a new museum is dedicated to the works of art themselves. The function of the museum has been radically extended and the public expect today's museum to be more than a series of rooms within which works of art are displayed. It must also be a centre of education and a place where temporary exhibitions can be put on in flexible open spaces. The shop and the restaurant have become essential features, while 'backstage'

the museum has to accommodate archival, laboratory and conservation areas.

The creation of the new wing obliged us to state the National Gallery's policy towards such changes and to say how far we thought they should affect the National Gallery. In our choice of architect, we felt that Venturi's ideas were fundamentally in sympathy with our own and that he provided the most satisfactory answers to the questions that we had asked ourselves. In the context of Trafalgar Square and the Wilkins building, we thought it right that the new building should not be too sharply contradictory. We welcomed its faces of fragmented classicism, and the Miesian modern glass wall through which the public would see the great staircase, both by day and at night.

We believe too that the right priorities were being established inside the building. With limited space available, the temporary exhibition rooms were to be situated in the basement of the building, with the lecture theatre also below ground level and the shop set to one side of the entrance hall. The rather low entrance hall entices the visitor towards the grand staircase, which looks backwards to the fifteenth century on one side but to the twentieth century on the other. It leads to the gallery floor with its surprising height and natural light, a design owing more to Sir John Soane and the Dulwich Picture Gallery than to any other influence. The 250 Early Renaissance paintings will probably be seen by more than 3.5 million visitors a year. As Venturi pointed out, at the time of Giotto the entire Italian peninsula had about the same number of inhabitants. Small in number the paintings may be, but in quality and range they are the equal of any public collection in the world. Bridget Riley, our artist Trustee until 1988, prepared a paper for the Trustees in December 1984, which began as follows:

The spirit of the National Gallery emanates from the paintings. Everything that has gone into the making of the works; the immense effort, the care and skill, the breadth and depth of feeling is reflected back to us. This is the *raison d'être* of the Gallery. Nothing should be allowed to tarnish or cloud this spirit and furthermore it should permeate the entire building, almost tangibly so.

If the new building upholds the values so admirably expressed by Bridget Riley, then a debt of gratitude is truly owed not only to our architect but also to many more individuals than I can possibly pay tribute to in this Foreword.

AUTHOR'S ACKNOWLEDGEMENTS

Distinguished new buildings are rare indeed in London and questions of approach and style will always and rightly be debated. We are confident that the building will be regarded as being as thoughtful and interesting architecturally as any created in London in the post-war period, and perhaps in some respects even more so. It is, we believe, a building of quality and distinction worthy of the collection that it will house. We are only able to have a happy and successful ending to our long and difficult story as a result of the Sainsbury brothers' great act of imaginative sponsorship, and I would like to conclude by congratulating and thanking John, Simon and Timothy Sainsbury once again. Their names have joined the other great benefactors of the National Gallery: Beaumont, Holwell-Carr, Salting, Layard, Lewis, Mond, Courtauld and J. Paul Getty Jr in our own time. They will have their permanent memorial in the building with which they have enriched this nation and which will stand as a proud landmark bearing their illustrious name.

Rothschild

LORD ROTHSCHILD *Chairman of the Trustees*

There are many people whose assistance has been invaluable in writing this book and to all of them I would like to express my gratitude. A number of people should be mentioned by name. Firstly I would like to thank the three donors, and in particular Simon Sainsbury, who has been consistently generous with his time and advice. The architects, Robert Venturi and Denise Scott Brown, have been hospitable and helpful throughout. David Vaughan and Steven Izenour, also of Venturi, Scott Brown and Associates, have helped considerably by providing essential material from their archives, and with photography; I am also indebted to their colleagues whose help and efficiency during my visits to Philadelphia have been greatly appreciated. At the National Gallery, Trustees and staff alike have provided insights and information at every stage. My thanks are due in particular to Jacob Rothschild, Caryl Hubbard, Michael Wilson, Eric Gabriel, Chris Watson, Grizelda Grimond and David Saunders; to Sara Hattrick, Astrid Athen, Colin Harvey, Colin White and Maria Conroy of the photographic department; and in the library to Elspeth Hector, Jacqueline McComish and Angelina Bacon. William Silver, Felicity Luard, Sue Curnow and Emma Shackleton of National Gallery Publications must be specially thanked for their work in producing this book. I would like to thank Peter Baistow for his design, Luci Collings for her editorial work, Paul Draper for his drawing of the Sainsbury Wing and Phil Starling for his fine photography. Finally I would like to thank Tom Price for his research and Matilda Palmer for all her help with the manuscript.

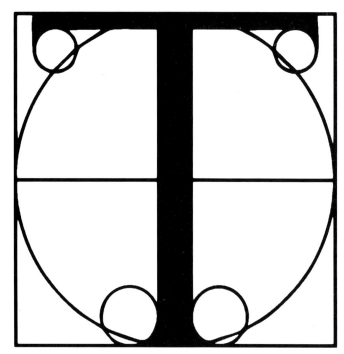

he opening of the Sainsbury Wing at the National Gallery is a time for celebration. It has taken a major and generous benefaction to develop the last remaining site in Trafalgar Square available for the expansion of the National Gallery. The public have been given a magnificent gift and London is much enriched by the galleries and facilities offered by the Sainsbury Wing, which completes the sequence of building devoted to art along the north side of Trafalgar Square, and elegantly and appropriately houses the earliest masterpieces of the national collection.

The completion of this last major addition to the National Gallery is the final chapter in a long story of debate, indecision, official prevarication and uncertainty concerning the housing of some of the nation's finest paintings. There seems to be something about the British character that is reluctant to commit national resources to the arts without an enormous fuss, public rows and Parliamentary explosions; a study of the archives shows that this has always been the case. The great mid-Victorian competitions did much to improve the quality of public buildings in the capital and concentrated the minds of architects, critics and the public alike on the 'battle of the styles'.

The National Gallery has always been at the centre of this debate, partly because of what it is, but also because of the very prominence of its position. It sits at one of the major crossroads of London, and it is the centrality of its site that has contributed to its popularity with Londoners. Free admission and a key location have meant that for several generations families have slipped in to see their favourite paintings. Of course the quality of the Collection is important, but the very fact that the Gallery dominates a great public square in the centre of London has made the place somewhere Londoners really care about, which is why so much attention has always been focused upon any changes to the building, particularly any proposals for major additions.

But the rows have not always been about architecture or the way that the national collection should be housed or hung: they have also been about the very nature of a national collection. Britain was late in the game of the establishment of a national gallery and this has, perhaps, coloured debates about its future and welfare. The idea was first mooted in 1777 when John Wilkes stood up in the House of Commons and urged that the nation should purchase Sir Robert Walpole's great collection of paintings from Houghton, before they were sold to Catherine the Great, Empress of Russia. Wilkes wanted

a national gallery to be built in the grounds of the British Museum, but his powerful advocacy was unsuccessful. In 1799 another collection was spurned when Noel Desenfans offered his paintings to the nation – his gift was later to become the basis of Dulwich Picture Gallery.

Perhaps the reasons that lay behind Britain's comparatively late acceptance of the idea of a national collection of paintings for the enlightenment of artists, students and the public were more philosophical than economic. John Constable was against the idea of a national gallery, claiming, in 1822, that 'There will be the end of the art in poor old England ... the manufacturers of pictures are made the criterion of perfection, instead of nature.' But Constable's voice was a lonely one. Many others were agitating for a national gallery, and the collector and connoisseur Sir George Beaumont was a powerful lobbyist from the 1820s. In 1823 he told the young Whig MP George Agar-Ellis that he would give his own pictures as soon as the Government could provide a home for them. The Prime Minister, Lord Liverpool, stalled on this occasion, again on the customary grounds of expense. But the battle for a gallery was taken up with greater vigour on the death of the financier John Julius Angerstein (1753–1823), who had formed a collection of paintings, including works by Raphael, Rembrandt and van Dyck, with the help and advice of the artist Thomas Lawrence. He housed his collection in a gallery in his home at 100 Pall Mall (the Reform Club now

stands on the site). Ministers were so nervous 'at Hume and the economists, that they could not bring themselves to make a decision', but on 2 April 1824 Parliament finally authorised the expenditure of £60,000 to buy 38 of Angerstein's pictures and the lease of the house in Pall Mall as the basis of a national gallery. This building, to which the public were admitted free of charge and provided with a cheap and simple catalogue, was ipso facto the first National Gallery. It was, after some debate, decided that it should be kept administratively separate from the British Museum. In 1826 it acquired Sir George Beaumont's collection of paintings, and five years later, in 1831, that of the Reverend Holwell Carr.

There was one campaigner for a national gallery, Agar-Ellis, who spoke fervently in Parliament of his hopes that the Government would 'erect a gallery which would be no less beneficial to the taste, than it would be conducive to the glory of the country.' He had felt strongly that any gift of paintings should not be consigned to 'the solitude of the British Museum', but that they must be 'situated in the very gangway of London where it is alike accessible and conveniently accessible to all ranks and degrees of men.' It is worth looking briefly, before embarking on the architectural history of the National Gallery and its latest extension, the Sainsbury Wing, at how the now familiar and affectionately regarded National Gallery building came to be situated at the 'very gangway of London'.

Above *Britain's first National Gallery opened in London on 10 May 1824 at 100 Pall Mall, the former town house of John Julius Angerstein. Thirty-eight pictures were purchased by the Government from Angerstein's heir to form the nucleus of the national collection. Anthony Trollope described the first home of the nation's pictures as 'a dingy, dull, narrow house, ill-adapted for the exhibition of the treasures it held.'*
Above left *The dense hang of pictures in Pall Mall attracted 24,000 visitors in the first seven months that it was open to the public.*
Top *The National Gallery of France already occupied the enormous galleries of the Louvre. This engraving was published in London to emphasise the contrasting levels of Government interest in the arts in England and France.*

HE BUILDING OF THE NATIONAL GALLERY

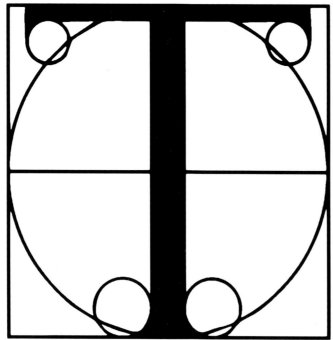

The neo-classical National Gallery, designed by William Wilkins in 1833, stands on the site of the old Royal Mews. Archaeological excavations that were carried out before construction began on the site of the Sainsbury Wing (to the west of Wilkins's building) uncovered some evidence of Saxon occupation. There was brief excitement at the discovery of three Saxon rubbish dumps, revealing pottery, oyster shells, coins and a few other artefacts. These finds appear to suggest that Saxon London extended considerably further west than had been previously thought.

It is believed to have been King Edward I who built the first Royal Mews on this important site that is the hinge on the route between the City of London and Westminster. The early mews buildings were originally the place of confinement for the royal hawks, falcons and kestrels while they were in moult or 'mewing'. The records of the Office of the King's Works show the presence of the paraphernalia of these sporting birds on this site in Charing Cross from 1273. In the time of King Henry VIII the Mews were partly pulled down, and a fire destroyed more in 1534. They were rebuilt as stables during the reign of Queen Elizabeth I. The seventeenth century saw the Mews being used for a variety of purposes including court lodgings and, later, for the housing of royalist prisoners after the Battle of Naseby. Following the Restoration, plans were made for the reconstruction of the Royal Mews, but elaborate proposals by Wren (there is a 'Plan for the Rebuilding the Royal Mews at Charing Cross' by Wren at All Souls College, Oxford) were never carried out. William Kent, however, did rebuild the stable block in 1732, exactly on the site where the National Gallery now stands. This, Kent's first work of official architecture, was carried out in accordance with a 'general plan' drawn up by the Board of Works.

Kent's 235-foot-long range was punctuated by a large and grand rusticated Doric archway and two cupolas reminis-

cent of the later Horse Guards in Whitehall. It was the arrival of this major public building that was first to prompt regular complaints about the lack in architectural quality of the surrounding neighbourhood. The Mews were encircled by a sea of banality, and even Gibbs's masterpiece, the magnificent portico and spire of the church of St Martin-in-the-Fields, was for a large part of its early life concealed by indifferent houses.

The improvements planned for London in the first two decades of the nineteenth century were accelerated by the reversion to the Crown of its Marylebone estate and by the need to link any new developments there to the centre of London. An Act of Parliament passed in 1813 to facilitate the construction of a new road through London, and the union of the offices of the Surveyor General of Land Revenue and the Surveyor General of Woods and Forests, made possible the adoption of John Nash's plan to link Carlton House with the new Regent's Park. The implementation of Nash's plan was eventually to provide London with a new square at Charing Cross and thus a suitable setting for a major new building to house the National Gallery.

In 1826 the Commissioner of HM Woods and Forests and Land Revenue published, in its fifth report, Nash's 1825 plan for the square. He had proposed on the north side (the site of the lower mews) a long, columned gallery for painting and sculpture, 460 feet in length, with domes and a central Corinthian portico. The most revolutionary proposal was for the erection in the middle of the new square of an almost precise copy of the Parthenon, which was to house the Royal

Academy, then bursting out of its cramped premises in Somerset House. On either side of this monumental edifice Nash suggested placing equestrian statues of King George III and King George IV. The report led to the Charing Cross Act of 1826 and superseded Nash's earlier plans, which had preserved the Royal Mews, taken Pall Mall around them, and indicated a new road from Charing Cross to the British Museum.

During the next few years both the Government and the Trustees of the National Gallery pondered a variety of solutions to the question of finding a home for the nation's paintings. There were proposals to extend the Pall Mall premises, to adapt

a part of the St James's Palace site or to convert the Royal Mews (plans to do this had, in fact, already been drawn up by Sydney Smirke).

It was the suggestion to convert the Mews that was to bring the architect William Wilkins into the picture. Wilkins was clearly a perceptive politician and he chose his moment well: he knew that Nash's influence was on the decline as a result of his recent extravagances at Buckingham Palace. Best known for his designs for the large and impressive University College, London, Wilkins was not yet the recipient of any Government patronage. He had failed to win the competition to design the Duke of York's column and for this he blamed the Leader of the Tory Party, the Duke of Wellington. This may have won him friends in the Whig regime of the day, and early in 1831 he approached Whig peers and MPs with his scheme for the conversion of the Royal Mews into a home for a combined National Gallery, Royal Academy and Public Records Office. The Treasury and the Gallery Trustees considered the plans that Wilkins had prepared but they felt that for an estimated sum of £35,000 they could probably fund the construction of a completely new building.

Early in 1832, Wilkins published a 'Letter to Lord Viscount Goderich' (written earlier) in which he advocated the idea of accessible art collections and encouraged patronage of native artists, arguing that the 'Fine Arts . . . essentially and abundantly contribute to the national prosperity and resources. It must be obvious that the present flourishing state of our manufacturers and export trade, is greatly due to the progress of the fine arts under His Majesty's Judicious Patronage . . . superior beauty and form have contributed to make our manufactures coveted throughout the world.' These views were very much in tune with the thinking of artists and dilettanti in the early decades of the nineteenth century. Wilkins, whose intervention had cut through several bureaucratic knots, was therefore asked to produce designs for the new gallery. The future, however, was not to be plain sailing for him. The 1828 report of the Select Committee on Public Buildings had advocated architectural competitions for official commissions, and so Charles Robert Cockerell and John Nash were also asked to submit proposals. Cockerell's design was a remarkable one, loosely based on the Pitti Palace with a 400-foot-long gallery above an arcaded base that was designed to contain shops. Nash's proposal, on the other hand, was for a long, colonnaded building with a large central portico. A Parliamentary Committee, chaired by Lord Duncannon, was established to consider the three proposed designs.

Below John Nash's plan for the development of Charing Cross prepared and presented to the House of Commons in 1826. It shows a long National Gallery of Painting and Sculpture to the north of the proposed square, and an oblong block in the centre of the square to house the Royal Academy.
Below right A plan of Trafalgar Square showing (shaded area) the outline of the buildings and courtyards that made up the Royal Mews in the eighteenth century.

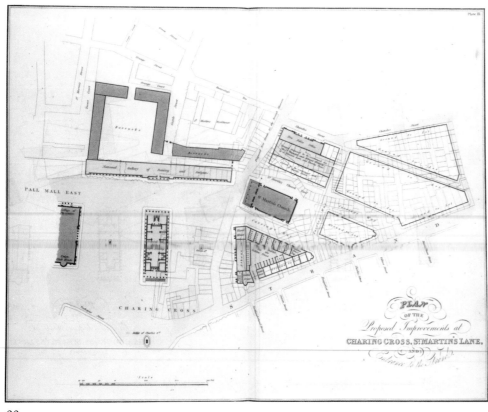

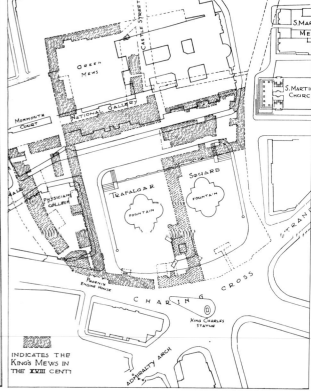

On 14 June 1832 Lord Duncannon's Committee decided to select Wilkins's design. It has to be said that the decision was taken largely on the grounds of economy – the Committee's report clearly stated that 'the objects sought for cannot be obtained by the public on terms more economical.' It was estimated that Cockerell's magnificent design would cost some £60,000 to build; Nash's designs to any committee now evoked worries of extravagance; Wilkins's proposal was estimated at £41,000, with some additional costs if more stone was used in the construction.

Government parsimony dogged the progress of Wilkins's proposal and many modifications were made before the plans were officially approved. His first scheme showed a building 461 feet long and 56 feet wide. The west wing was designed to house the Public Record Office on the ground floor and there was a vaulted passage to ensure a right of way through the building to the barracks behind, as well as to Duke Court and Castle Street. Wilkins used cast iron for fireproofing and introduced some other innovations, including traps in the floors for the hoisting of large paintings, and proposed the use of the drum of the dome as a drawing studio for Royal Academy students (the Royal Academy was to occupy the east wing). He was, however, forced to move the line of his building some 50 feet to the north to give a view of the long-hidden portico of St

Martin-in-the-Fields. This clearly upset Wilkins, who revealed an architectural arrogance in his comments on the quality of Gibbs's work. Looking at the portico he is reputed to have said: 'I should have passed a great many years of useless study if I could not design something very superior. . . .' It was also suggested that he should raise the height of his building by five feet to match the cornice of St Martin-in-the-Fields. This proposal (which would have been a considerable improvement to the low-slung design) was subsequently abandoned because tenders were too high, and it was agreed to raise the building by only one foot.

By August of 1833 the estimates for Wilkins's revised design came to £66,000, less £4,000 for reused materials – for example the columns from the recently demolished Carlton House. This figure did not include commission on tenders and once again the project was considered too expensive and appeared to be threatened. Lord Duncannon suggested to Parliament that perhaps they might consider converting the Banqueting House in Whitehall into a gallery. By September, undoubtedly after considerable anxious pressure from the architect himself, Wilkins's plan (literally with its wings clipped), received the go ahead. Later that month King William IV signed the plans at the Royal Academy and building work commenced.

Building lasted for almost five years and throughout the period Wilkins was the target of endless criticism and murmurings of discontent. It was not only the architect who was criticised, the Government too was rightly upbraided for its

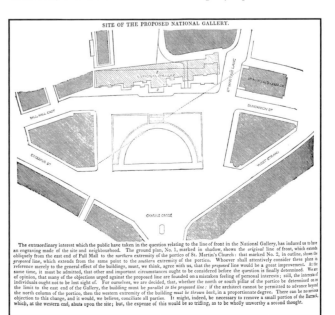

SITE OF THE PROPOSED NATIONAL GALLERY.

The extraordinary interest which the public have taken in the question relating to the line of front in the National Gallery, has induced us to have an engraving made of the site and neighbourhood. The ground plan, No. 1, marked in shadow, shows the *original* line of front, which extends obliquely from the east end of Pall Mall to the *northern* extremity of the portico of St. Martin's Church: that marked No. 2, in outline, shows the *proposed* line, which extends from the same point to the *southern* extremity of the portico. Whoever shall attentively consider these plans in reference merely to the general effect of the buildings, must, we think, agree with us, that the *proposed* line would be a great improvement. At the same time, it must be admitted, that other and important circumstances ought to be considered before the question is finally determined. We are of opinion, that many of the objections urged against the proposed line are founded on a mistaken feeling of personal interests; still, the interests of individuals ought not to be lost sight of. For ourselves, we are decided, that, whether the north or south pillar of the portico be determined on as the limit to the east end of the Gallery, the building must be *parallel to the proposed line:* if the architect cannot be permitted to advance beyond the north column of the portico, then the western extremity of the building must be *thrown back,* in a proportionate degree. There can be no serious objection to this change, and it would, we believe, conciliate all parties. It might, indeed, be necessary to remove a small portion of the Barrack, which, at the western end, abuts upon the site; but, the expense of this would be so trifling, as to be wholly unworthy of a second thought.

Opposite top *Wilkins's design as published in* The Athenaeum *in 1834 showing the 'sculptural enrichment' he planned so that the 'effect of the buildings would thus be prodigiously heightened.' The ground plan* (beneath) *shows the main floor – the east wing was to be occupied by the Royal Academy.*

Below *Detail of one of the two openings in the façade which Wilkins called his 'propylaea', with one of his proposed sculptural groups on the skyline. The sculpture, by his friend Royal Academician Charles Rossi, was not in fact executed.*

parsimony. The building process was a curious one, with work starting at either end of the new gallery in order to allow the public records stored at the centre of the site in the old Mews to remain in place during the first phase of construction. Early in 1835 the records could be moved and Parliament, with some degree of reluctance, voted an extra £12,000 for the building of the central section.

Poor Wilkins was criticised for everything. There were complaints that there had been no real competition. There were complaints about the architectural style, and a vicious campaign was mounted by certain critics to use the National Gallery design as evidence of the terminal decline of the Greek Revival. Faced with judgments like that of the *Literary Gazette*, which in 1833 called the design 'altogether incompetent and ridiculous . . . half barbarous, half Grecian, half Gothic', and the *Architectural Magazine* of 1834, which criticised the lack of stylistic unity in the elevation and expressed the view that it should have been bigger and bolder, Wilkins struggled to defend himself. Perhaps foolishly he attacked his critics on architectural grounds and did not place sufficient emphasis on the incredibly low budget and Government prevarication. It did not help his case when he announced that his National Gallery design was 'the pure basis of Grecian excellence', adding that 'I cannot sacrifice what I feel to be true, at the shrine of humility.'

It should be remembered that Wilkins had wanted to design a building with a monumentality appropriate to the magnificent setting. He knew that his building for University College had much greater strength, and that his National Gallery would be judged alongside Smirke's British Museum and other grand continental examples such as the Glyptothek (1816–34) in Munich by Leo von Klenze, and Karl Friedrich Schinkel's great neo-classical Altes Museum (1823–30) in Berlin, with its continuous row of Ionic columns on the main façade. Perhaps Wilkins had this last in mind when he wrote in his *Proclusiones Architectonicae* of 1837 that 'Every portico whether in the end or in the centre of a long range . . . should be or appear to be the ornamental termination of two flank walls.'

Even while his design was being built Wilkins suffered from the publication of an alternative design that was promoted by Sir Charles Barry (in association with Sir Edward Cust) as part of a Parliamentary Commission on the National Gallery. This showed a much loftier building that dominated the proposed Trafalgar Square more effectively than Wilkins's creation. Wilkins has always been criticised for designing a façade that is much too low for the great square that it confronts. However, it must be remembered that he was forced to build under the stringent conditions imposed by the Government, and what we see today is as much a monument to expediency as anything else. (Interestingly enough, during the recent competition for the Hampton site extension, the architect Roderick Gradidge published a scheme to add two tall side wings and a grand central dome to Wilkins's building in such a way as to give it the prominence it should always have displayed in town-planning terms.)

Wilkins staked his career on the National Gallery. By arguing for a temple of the arts he did succeed (with others) in dissuading the powers that be from simply converting an existing building into some semblance of a national institution. However, what would we now think of Wilkins's Gallery if he had also secured the commission to lay out Trafalgar Square, with a broad flight of steps leading up to his portico? Wilkins regarded his proposals for the square as 'essential to the general effect of the buildings'. His roads and terraces would undoubtedly have helped to bind together the disparate buildings around the space and there is no doubt that his design would have substantially elevated his building. But he pleaded in vain for his scheme, for some 'common justice to the architect, who relied for the effect of the whole upon a point so important and who had been so unjustly made the subject of attack and vituperation by those who have seen the building carried on in divisions and who have never considered the effect of the WHOLE design as originally intended.'

As part of the process of building a public edifice for the Government, Wilkins had to endure examination by the Select Committee on Arts and Manufactures. Once again he was strongly criticised on almost all fronts, only his top lighting and his gallery plan were respected. One member of the Committee, Samuel Woodburn, a connoisseur, defended Wilkins and rightly placed much of the blame for the shortcomings of the gallery where they belonged:

I wish, equally with Mr Wilkins, that the space had been five times as large, and then he could have made something which would have been more worthy of the country. I should say that owing to the public outcry, Mr Wilkins has not made the best that could be made, but his being urged as he was by the public voice to curtail it, has been a misfortune.

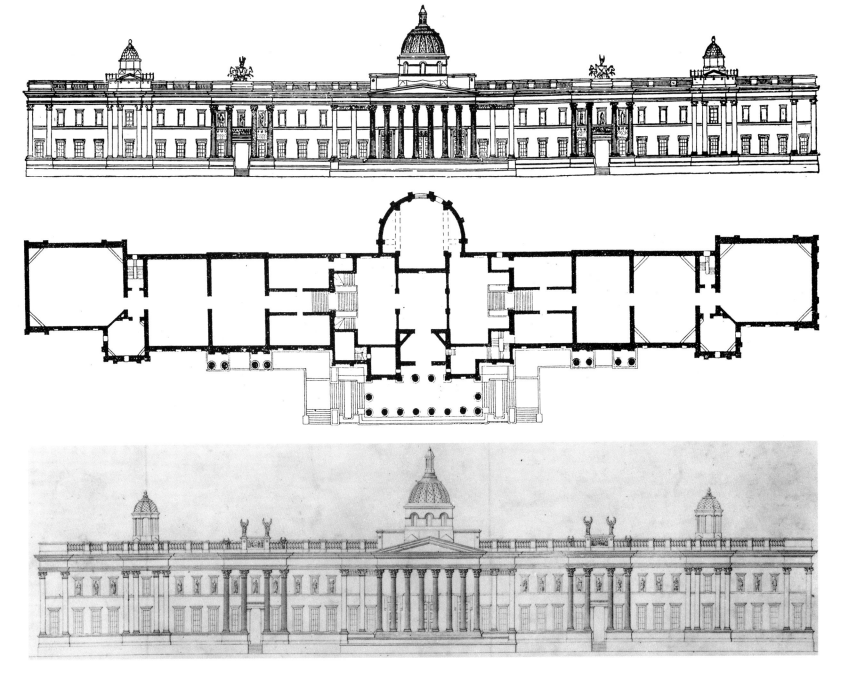

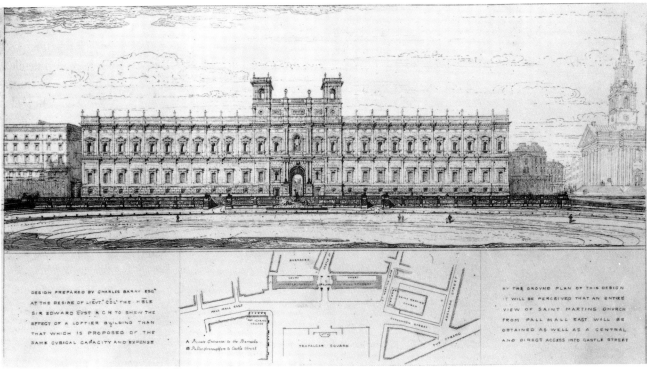

Above *Wilkins's 1835 modification of the main façade, which now has a series of sculptures in niches, and on the balustrade to break the long horizontal roofline.*

Left *Charles Barry's alternative Neo-Renaissance design that was published by Colonel Sir Edward Cust MP in the* Literary Gazette *of 1833 to induce the Government to persuade Wilkins to design a higher building that would dominate the new square.*

25

26

An idealised view of the newly completed gallery. Wilkins hoped that his long façade would face onto a new square of his own design, but it was to be Charles Barry who won the commission to lay out the square, and William Railton who added the giant Corinthian column in 1842 to honour the memory of Admiral Lord Nelson. Sir Edwin Lutyens later remodelled Barry's fountains beside Landseer's lions in the 1930s.

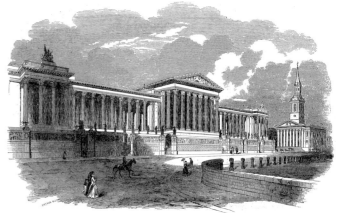

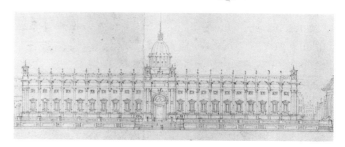

Above *An engraving showing Railton's proposal for Nelson's Column, drawn about 1840.*
Bottom right *HM Queen Victoria visits the Royal Academy in the new Wilkins building.*

On 28 April 1837 King William IV opened the new galleries. The following year, on 7 April, Queen Victoria visited the Gallery to see the newly hung paintings, and the National Gallery was opened to the public two days later. Wilkins died at the end of August 1839, his health probably weakened by the constant barrage of criticism and the bad press following the opening of his building. The sad truth is that he was so circumscribed by interference and budgetary conditions that it made it impossible for him to build a gallery of international stature. The architectural critic and scholar James Fergusson was later to put the whole problem into perspective when he wrote in his *History of the Modern Styles* (1862):

> We know that Wilkins had talent enough to erect a creditable building if he had had fair play; but the public thought proper to impose conditions which rendered his doing so next to impossible. The sad result to the architect is well known; but on a fair review of the circumstances it does not appear that he was to blame for the painful result in Trafalgar Square.

The bad press that greeted the opening of the Gallery was to

continue for years afterwards. The shortcomings of Wilkins's building were to be constantly aired and alternative proposals put forward. There were serious drawbacks. There was never enough space. There was no conservation room. The whole building was dusty, ill-ventilated and inefficiently heated by open fireplaces. As Nelson's Column rose in the new square so new plans to improve, or even replace, the National Gallery were regularly published. As early as 1838, John and Sebastian Gwilt (their father, Joseph, is better known as a writer on

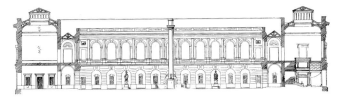

antiquarian and architectural subjects; Sebastian was an architect who also illustrated his father's *Encyclopaedia of Architecture*, 1842) prepared elaborate proposals for a new National Gallery on the site of Trafalgar Square. They argued that Nash's square was 'an enormous vacant area of no utility', and that their own new gallery would not only have

room for the largest paintings, but would also provide a range of commercial arcades housing shops that would bring in an income. When it came to architectural style, they declared, 'it would have no needless display of columns not performing any useful office.'

In 1845 Charles Locke Eastlake (then second Keeper of the National Gallery, and in 1855 its first Director) published in *The Builder* a letter he had written to Sir Robert Peel on the general unfitness of the National Gallery. He suggested enlarging the Wilkins building or moving the Gallery to new premises on an open site to allow for future expansion. Questions were asked in the House of Commons, and a pamphlet written by George Russell French proposed rehousing the Collection in Buckingham Palace and building a new residence for the monarch. Additional space was badly needed. Because of the acute overcrowding of the works, the Vernon Bequest of 1847 and the Turner Bequest of 1856 had to be stored, along with other British paintings, in Marlborough House, left vacant on the death of the Queen Dowager, Queen Adelaide. In addition about a thousand paintings and drawings were temporarily housed in the South Kensington Museum.

ALTERNATIVE PROPOSALS Opposite
Proposals to alter the National Gallery put forward by (from the top) *Henry Ashton in 1848; an unknown designer (watercolour from the Museum of London); Arthur Allom in 1849 – whose giant Corinthian-columned façade rises above a high plinth; and a design possibly by Charles Barry, c. 1835–48.* Left *John and Sebastian Gwilt's 1838 proposal (transverse section) for a new National Gallery.* Above *One of the earliest daguerreotypes of London, taken in 1839, showing Wilkins's Gallery.*

April 6, 1861.] THE BUILDER. 231

NATIONAL GALLERY, LONDON: THE NEW ROOM.—Mr. James Pennethorne, Architect.

Top left *In 1861 James Pennethorne added a large new room to the Gallery, which replaced the entrance stairs designed by Wilkins* (top right).

Above *The artist David Roberts made some grandiose designs for a new National Gallery in 1856. He claimed 'who so fit as a painter to design such an Edifice?'*

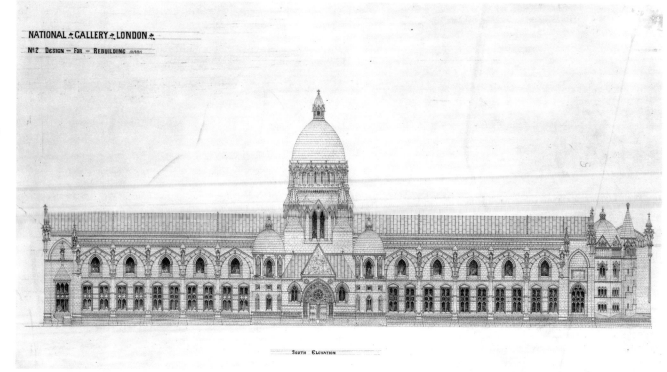

NATIONAL ⁂ GALLERY ⁂ LONDON ⁂

No 2 DESIGN — FOR — REBUILDING

SOUTH ELEVATION

During the 1850s a series of select committees considered the future of the National Gallery and several architects published proposals. The removal of the Royal Academy from its shared premises offered the easiest solution, but there were many advocates for the relocation of the whole Gallery to South Kensington. Henry Cole was enthusiastic for a private venture, remarking with some degree of truth that 'private enterprise works more efficiently than government in carrying out such enterprises.' In December 1856 the National Gallery Site Commission was set up to examine the whole question of a move or the possible amalgamation of the National Gallery with the art and architecture department of the British Museum. Finally, in February 1866, a competition was held to design a new National Gallery. The 'Instructions to Architects' distributed by the Office of Works requested designs for alternative solutions. An Act of Parliament in 1866 provided 'for the acquisition of a site for the enlargement of the National Gallery', although there was opposition to the selling of the barracks on the adjoining site, particularly from the Duke of Cambridge, Commander in Chief, and uncle of Queen Vic-

toria. Competitors were invited to submit proposals for the best way of laying out the new site and were given the option of 'retaining the existing building' (without the occupancy of the Royal Academy in the eastern portion), or of 'reconstructing or remodelling it' – this second alternative being taken to mean that Wilkins's building could be demolished. There was a request that the largest possible extent of hanging space should be achieved in a manner that was 'consistent with grand architectural effects'. Top lighting was preferred but side light was acceptable for cabinet pictures and drawings. A committee of nine judges was appointed, including two architects, the President of the Royal Institute of British Architects, A. J. B. Beresford-Hope (who was also an MP), and David Brandon. The ten architects who submitted designs were: Owen Jones, Cuthbert Brodrick, George Edmund Street, Frederick Pepys Cockerell, James Murray, Edward Middleton Barry, Francis Cranmer Penrose, George Somers Clarke, Matthew Digby Wyatt, and the firm of Banks and Barry (Charles Barry junior).

We have become familiar today with architectural competitions that somehow fail to satisfy anyone. The worst sort of

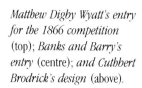

competition, although in theory one that should produce the goods, is the completely open competition. Everyone hopes for a *deus ex machina* to appear in such a competition and produce a masterpiece, but this very seldom happens. Competitions, to be effective, need very precise and full briefs. On this occasion the entrants definitely suffered from an inadequate brief. Perhaps not unsurprisingly the competition did not produce a winner. Curiously, before the judges had made any decision, the designs were exhibited during January 1867 in the Royal Gallery of the Palace of Westminster. The judges gave their report at the end of February, declaring no-one the winner. They praised Edward Middleton Barry's design for a new gallery and James Murray's scheme for adaptation. Both of these they felt showed 'the greatest amount of architectural merit'. The First Commissioner of Works, commenting on the outcome, wrote that 'the main cause of want of success in the design was that complete and accurate instructions were not given to the architects.'

Historically, it is probably right to judge the National Gallery competition alongside that for the Law Courts, as both

took place in the same year and both influenced the future of British public buildings. The Law Courts competition produced a grand and fantastic series of great gothic designs. Some of the finest schemes of the nineteenth century were drawn for these Royal Courts of Justice and yet the result of the competition was initially confusing and apparently arbitrary. Joint winners were named – George Edmund Street for his severe thirteenth-century gothic elevations and Edward Middleton Barry for his immaculate planning. Alfred Waterhouse's glorious panorama of towers was also much admired. Predictably, however, the joint winners found it difficult to work together and by the end of May 1868 Street had been made the sole architect of the Law Courts; in June Barry was named as the architect of the new National Gallery. A letter from the Office of Works to E. M. Barry clearly linked the two competitions in the judges' minds: 'It was upon a consideration of all the circumstances attending the National Gallery and the Law Courts, that your appointment took place.'

Barry was unhappy with the outcome and his remarks reveal that he felt that the National Gallery building (perhaps

because of its chequered past) was very much the lesser commission. He wrote that he thought the Gallery 'the lesser work' and was upset that the decision should 'refuse me the opportunity of obtaining lasting fame and advantages, by having my name connected with the largest and most important public building of the age.'

It was in October 1868 that Barry was asked for his plans for the rebuilding. The question of style had been raised in the House but, as a modern commentator, H. Grubert, has observed, 'it was assumed as a matter of course that some adaptation of Classic or Renaissance architecture is the only style allowable for museums and picture galleries. Of all the entries for the Law Courts competition only one was Classical and of the entries for the National Gallery only two were Gothic.' Barry was far from overjoyed at the prospect; fearing the worst he wrote that he would 'merely be adding one patch to an already mutilated and condemned building'. It seems that his original submission for the 1866 competition was considered extravagant. His great staircase was described by the author of the Works Department Report as 'a splendid example

Frederick Pepys Cockerell's entry for the 1866 competition (top), *and Francis Cranmer Penrose's entry* (above).

Opposite *E. M. Barry's entry for the 1866 competition, and his grand interior – looking from the southwest loggia to the west gallery.*

of architectural design [which] occupies the whole of the centre of the building . . . . I do not know anything so magnificent, but I cannot but consider it as wholly misplaced in this instance.' But Barry's appointment was official and he had the chance to visit the newer museums in Europe and to prepare plans for a new gallery that could be built in stages.

A new First Commissioner of Works, A. S. Ayrton, who had been a Parliamentary Secretary to the Treasury, was appointed in 1869. Ayrton made it plain in public that he was opposed to any expenditure of state money on the arts, and he was to make life difficult for Barry through constant cost-cutting. He was responsible for the lack of any decision about Barry's design and, in fact, he and the Treasury killed off any idea of a new National Gallery by asking Barry for plans for an *extension* only (the Royal Academy had eventually moved to its new home in 1869, releasing more space for the Gallery.) It is not known how the news was conveyed to Barry that he was, after all, only being asked to add eight galleries to Wilkins's building, but he seems to have been treated extremely unreasonably. In 1870 Barry wrote that 'no pecuniary consideration could be regarded as . . . compensation for losing the hard-won opportunity of earning lasting fame and reputation by connecting my name with the great national work of the new National Gallery.' It is easy to understand the chronic sense of disappointment that he must have felt when the terrific labour of winning such a prestigious competition seemed to have been in vain. Barry was quite certain where the blame lay. Much later, in a lecture to the Royal Academy in 1879, he said, 'We can scarcely expect again to have great architectural triumphs if the question about any important public work is . . . how little can it be made to cost?'

The Barry Rooms were opened in August 1876. With their high dome they made quite a showing on the exterior of the National Gallery above the long Wilkins façade. Barry had provided some eight new galleries, with offices and conservation studios below, on the plot of land behind the eastern side of Wilkins's building. They were and are handsome rooms, although they have had their critics. They are highly decorative, with double columns of green Genoan marble on black Belgian marble plinths. Representations of Architecture, Painting and Sculpture and a head of Queen Victoria fill plaster lunettes, and there was originally a gilded inscription around the dome. The words were those of Sir Joshua Reynolds: 'The works of those who have stood the test of ages have a claim to that respect and veneration to which no modern can pretend.'

ADDITIONS TO THE NATIONAL GALLERY.—Professor E. M. Barry, R.A., Architect.   [See p. 725.

THE BARRY ROOMS
Left *The central hall of the new suite of rooms added to the Gallery by E. M. Barry, as illustrated in* The Builder *in July 1876.*
Opposite below *Painting by Giovanni Gabrielli of E. M. Barry's new rooms soon after they opened in 1876, showing the richness of the decorative scheme and the crowded arrangement of pictures.*

Below left *The new stair hall and vestibule designed for the National Gallery in 1884 by Sir John Taylor for the Office of Works.*
Below *The 1911 fireproof extension of the National Gallery, showing the interior of the new west gallery.*

The Builder magazine wrote at the time that 'a weaker inscription could not have been found.' When the Barry Rooms were restored in the 1980s it was not reinstated. As always there was criticism and some of the Gallery Trustees disliked the decorations and colours chosen by Barry, lamenting 'the dominance of architectural adornment and profane polychrome decoration which distinguishes these rooms, where ornament and colour, though perhaps not necessarily out of place, have in this instance been most injudiciously applied.' In 1879 the Government formally told Barry that they had abandoned any intention of rebuilding the National Gallery.

Although the Gallery now had 20 rooms for the display of paintings, more space was soon needed and in 1884 the Office of Works passed plans for a new stair hall, vestibule and five more galleries by their own architect, Sir John Taylor. These rooms were opened in 1887 and were distinguished by their decoration by John Crace: deep-red flock wallpapers, dark green friezes with a stone fret pattern and the rest of the entablature embellished with bronze and gilding.

But the Gallery Trustees continued to ask the Treasury for more space and urged the acquisition of the adjoining barracks – particularly as the site to the east, which the National Gallery had hoped for, was acquired for the National Portrait Gallery in 1890. The risk of fire from neighbouring buildings was frequently mentioned as a serious hazard and a fire in Watherston's shop, which faced onto what is now Jubilee Walk, between the Gallery and Hampton's premises to the west, caused serious concern. It wasn't until 1901 that the barracks were cleared, and in 1902 Watherston's shop was demolished.

In 1911 five further galleries were added by the Office of Works to the west side of the building. Sir Joseph Duveen was the donor of another fine gallery, which was opened in 1927 to house Sir Hugh Lane's collection, left to the Gallery in 1918; a room was later added for the Mond Bequest. By now the Trustees had partially succeeded in consolidating the Gallery's position on as much of the Trafalgar Square site as could be secured. They had not, however, been able to acquire the Hampton site, although at the time of the Second World War the Gallery's Director, Kenneth Clark, had exciting plans for the use of the site to house the paintings that he had persuaded Calouste Gulbenkian to pledge to the nation. Plans for a building on the Hampton site were drawn up by the American architect William Delano, but the Gulbenkian Bequest was ultimately withdrawn. It was to take another 50 years for the Hampton site to be fully utilised by the National Gallery.

CHAPTER 2

OMMERCE AND COMPETITIONS

The Hampton site was for some years after the Second World War seen as the natural, and indeed the only, place where the National Gallery could expand. During the war Hampton's building was bombed some six times. On the sixth occasion, in November 1940, it was hit by a high explosive bomb and gutted by fire. Mercifully, the nation's pictures were secure in the Manod slate quarries in remotest Wales. Hampton's held some of the site on a Crown lease and some of it freehold. In 1955 the Canadian Government – the National Gallery's neighbour in Canada House on the west side of Trafalgar Square – bought out Hampton's and took on the Crown lease. The old idea (which had emerged over the years) of an imperial precinct of buildings around Trafalgar Square housing the representative governments of former colonial territories had never been completely abandoned. Sir Herbert Baker's South Africa House (1935) stands opposite Canada House (1824–7), and New Zealand was to build on Pall Mall East (1957–63). There was also a plan for an official Commonwealth House on the Hampton site, which was to be combined with a small extension for the National Gallery.

But it was not the manoeuvrings of Commonwealth governments that delayed the acquisition of the site for the National Gallery – it was the old story of Treasury caution and Government reluctance to spend money on the arts. In 1958, following the Royal Fine Art Commission's rejection of the Canadian Government's scheme to build additional offices on the Hampton site, the Chairman of the Gallery Trustees, Lionel Robbins, wrote to *The Times* urging that this strategic site be kept for the future use of either the National Gallery or the National Portrait Gallery – a proposal that was supported by a press campaign. A developer, Samuel Sebba, commissioned the architect Donald McMorran to produce a scheme with which to negotiate for the acquisition of the entire site from the Canadian Government. Interestingly enough this was the first ever scheme to propose a combination of commercial development and gallery space. Sebba wrote to McMorran arguing that 'there is no doubt that the combined project could pro-

duce a most striking and distinguished effect.' Lionel Robbins was not slow to comment, calling the scheme 'deplorably of the order of the fourth best'.

Lobbying and plotting over the site continued during 1958 until the Government was persuaded to buy it in the November of that year, having announced in the House of Commons that it 'felt it to be undesirable that normal commercial development should take place on this site.' The Government spokesman was unwilling to say when it would be used for a new National Gallery building. Instead, he emphasised how much it had cost to repair the National Gallery after the war and explained that some £700,000 would be spent on reconstruction and air conditioning. The Government would let the site for some 20 to 25 years, with a view to future development. Sebba, undaunted, produced a second plan to build a new gallery on the site, which he planned to adapt and use as offices for 25 years, after which time he would hand it back to the Gallery. This came to nothing.

Public attention was now focused on the Hampton site,

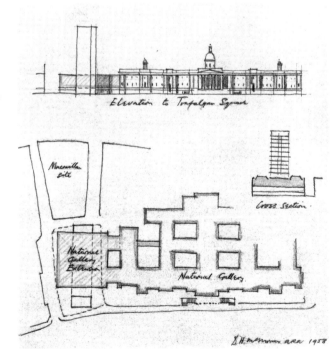

Above *During the Second World War the Hampton building was bombed six times. The sixth time was in November 1940, when a high explosive bomb caused it to be gutted by fire.*
Left *In 1958 a developer proposed a combination of commercial development and gallery space; the plan included a tower block of offices to be designed by Donald McMorran.*

THE NATIONAL GALLERY CONTROVERSY

Sir Albert looks at The Sunday Times prizewinners and makes his own choice

Reaction to the announcement of the prizewinners in "The Sunday Times" £5,000 competition for the development of the National Gallery site has been immediate and controversial. While many readers acclaim the winning designs, many others are strongly opposed to the "modernism" they feel most of the competing architects have shown.

Robert Harling went with Sir Albert Richardson, Past President of the Royal Academy and Professor of Architecture at the Royal Academy Schools, to the exhibition of the winning designs at the Building Centre and here reports the views of one of the leading exponents of traditionalism in British architecture.

By ROBERT HARLING

SIR ALBERT RICHARDSON, unlike most traditionalists, attacks the others. To him this isn't just the so-called best method of defence ; he sincerely thinks that the kind of building "now calling itself architecture" needs attacking. All the time. "If we do this," he says, "we can still save England."

And so he came to the Building Centre for the exhibition of designs for THE SUNDAY TIMES National Gallery Competition.

He arrived in splendidly traditional style: Rolls-Royce, bowler hat, rolled umbrella.

"I saw the designs in last

THE WINNING ARCHITECT'S OWN PERSPECTIVE
Since we published Dennis Flanders's perspective drawings of the prizewinning designs last Sunday, we have received from architect Barrie Dewhurst, the prizewinner, now working in Boston, U.S.A., his own perspective drawing of his projected design.

MODEL OF THE SECOND-PRIZE DESIGN
The photograph above shows a model of the design by Boissevain & Osmond, which gained second prize in the competition.

THE SUNDAY TIMES 1959 COMPETITION
Above *Barrie Dewhurst's winning design for* The Sunday Times *1959 competition, and the model designed by the second prizewinners – Boissevain and Osmond.*
Right *Third prize was won by I. H. and R. P. Marshall (top).* William Crabtree *(middle) and* Mervyn Handley *(bottom) won joint fourth prize.*

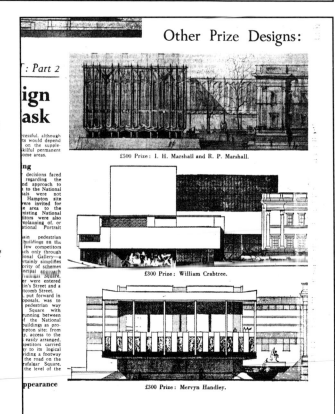

Other Prize Designs:

: Part 2

ign ask

...cessful, although ...ts would depend ...on the supple- ...kilful permanent ...ome areas.

...ng

...decisions faced ...regarding the ...nd approach to ...to the National ...als were not ...Hampton site ...ere invited for ...e area to the ...xisting National ...itors were also ...eplanning of, or ...ional Portrait

...ain pedestrian ...buildings on the ...few competitors ...ch only through ...onal Gallery—a ...rtainly simplifies ...ority of schemes ...ncipal approach ...Trafalgar Square, ...er were entered ...ain's Street and a ...tcomb Street. ...put forward in ...oposals, was to ...pedestrian way ...Square with ...running between ...f the National ...buildings as pro- ...npton site: from ...y, access to the ...easily arranged. ...petitors carried ...y to its logical ...iding a footway ...the road on the ...rafalgar Square, ...the level of the

...ppearance

£500 Prize: I. H. Marshall and R. P. Marshall.

£300 Prize: William Crabtree.

£300 Prize: Mervyn Handley.

although there were no guarantees that it would be used for the National Gallery. Indeed, it was often considered more likely that the National Portrait Gallery would build itself a new home on the site and that the National Gallery would expand into the old National Portrait Gallery premises and other spaces at the back of the two galleries. It was *The Sunday Times* that further encouraged public interest in the dilemma by launching a major architectural competition in January 1959. Offering £5,000 in prize money, the organisers announced that they were staging 'a competition of ideas rather than a search for a solution to a programme of specific requirements'. Limited to the Hampton site, the competition attracted some 1,400 initial registrations and 252 actual designs from British and Commonwealth entrants. The assessors on this occasion were a high-powered team: Sir William Holford (later to become Lord Holford) was in the 1950s distinguished as a town planner and responsible for the plans of the Paternoster precinct to the northeast of St Paul's Cathedral; Peter Chamberlain, as a partner in the firm Chamberlain, Powell and Bon, was responsible for the City of London's Barbican development; and William Allen was superintending architect at the Building Research Station. It is often said that if you look at the judges for a competition you can foresee the result. In this case it was clear that an uncompromisingly modern building, probably built of concrete and influenced by Le Corbusier, would be the winner. The assessors said in their report that they were looking for an idea 'which is, and will be most central to the whole intention of extending the National Galleries, that is to say the creation of a new series of spaces for exhibiting the national collections, in which there would be' – in the words of the competition brief – 'good visual conditions and generally enjoyable circumstances for the viewers, a place, in other words with a sense of occasion, complementary to the existing building, and not just a repetition of it.'

There was one outright winner and three runners-up, with eight winners of £50 prizes and 48 recommended schemes. The top four were: first, Barrie Dewhurst; second, Boissevain and Osmond; third, I. H. and R. P. Marshall; and equal fourth, Mervyn Handley and William Crabtree. The winning scheme – inspired by both Frank Lloyd Wright and Le Corbusier – was designed by Barrie Dewhurst, a 38-year-old product of the Architectural Association who, at the time of the competition, was working in America. The assessors particularly admired the horizontality of his design and its apparently

clever plan of a squared spiral of galleries rising up to the level of the main floor of the Wilkins building. Dewhurst's building – constructed from what appeared to be shuttered concrete – looked like a chest of drawers with various drawers pulled out and left open at random. It was described by the *Architects' Journal* as 'in purely abstract spatial terms, undoubtedly the most distinguished and richly developed design of any . . .'. The second prizewinner, by Boissevain and Osmond, was very different – a solid rectangular box on pilotis, set back on a sculpture terrace. There was to be a two-storey glass link to Wilkins's building. In third place, I. H. and R. P. Marshall had produced a rather remarkable scheme, and one that was very much of the 1950s. With its roof of glass prisms and its feel of a glass tent, it had something of the spirit of the Festival of Britain about it. The interior clearly excited the assessors: 'the entrance leads over water, to a great oval staircase and to galleries like haunted ballrooms made even more mysterious by suspended screens.'

The winning entries were all put on public exhibition and generated considerable comment – although not everyone was inspired by the winning design. Sir Albert Richardson, Professor of Architecture at the Royal Academy, was grateful to *The Sunday Times* for showing the public 'the kind of thing they've got to guard against'. Gresham Cooke MP declared in the House of Commons that 'most people would think it a deplorable blight on London if *The Sunday Times* winning design was chosen.'

The competition produced several other extremely interesting designs, all of which in some way or another exposed the problems of building an extension on the Hampton site. Many of the entrants, for example, had made intelligent suggestions for linking Trafalgar and Leicester Squares, as well as producing ideas for an underground link from the Gallery to the fountains in the middle of Trafalgar Square. It's worth looking at these earlier designs as a prelude to a consideration of the Sainsbury Wing, for the architects Venturi, Scott Brown and Associates from Philadelphia faced exactly the same problems nearly 30 years later.

The key problem has always been to achieve large, top-lit galleries on the same level as the main floor of galleries in Wilkins's building, while fully utilising the space on the narrow Hampton site. The configuration of the site makes understandable the later decision of the Government and the Trustees of the National Gallery to try and pay for new galleries by designating the whole of the lower half of any building for commercial use. This would never have been an ideal option, but the awkward site is hard to use effectively for gallery purposes as only the very top floor can enjoy natural light from above (side lighting from windows posing considerable viewing problems). The requirement of *The Sunday Times* competition for some 15,000 square feet of air-conditioned, top-lit gallery space posed the problem of how to circulate the Gallery visitors up to a floor some 25 or 30 feet above street level. A multistorey building is inevitable, given the nature of the site, and it is the progression of the visitor from street to gallery level that at once poses architectural problems and offers exciting possibilities for devising views of Trafalgar Square and an enjoyable sequence of architectural movement.

In this 1959 competition the assessors thought that it was important for the 'form of the new building to contrast – but not conflict – with the existing National Gallery'. It is significant that the majority of winning and commended

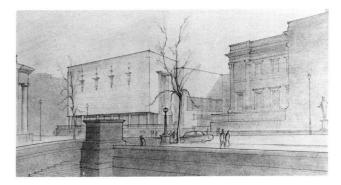

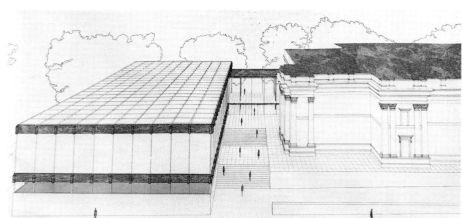

entries followed Wilkins's building in scale and height. However, the architectural climate was not averse to more radical solutions, and the *Architects' Journal* considered that the possibility of a tower block above the galleries was a viable proposition. The real value of *The Sunday Times* competition, though, was in terms of propaganda. It showed how the Hampton site could be used by the National Gallery and also demonstrated some of the architectural difficulties posed by expansion. It is fair to say that the winning design did not particularly stir the public imagination, and lack of funds probably saved the National Gallery from having to show some of its finest pictures in a series of concrete spaces resembling the Mappin Terraces at London Zoo.

The years following the competition saw renewed pressure for the National Gallery to expand, not onto the Hampton site but into the rooms occupied by the National Portrait Gallery – with the National Portrait Gallery eventually occupying its own new, self-contained building on the Hampton site. But in October 1960 the Chancellor of the Exchequer refused any grant of funds for a new gallery and so began the sorry saga of the empty Hampton site, leased in October 1961 and used as a car park. It was to be nearly 30 years before it would become the site of a magnificent extension of the National Gallery.

There were, however, some architectural developments within the National Gallery itself during this period. The Gallery's northern extension was started in 1970, providing ten new public galleries (which increased the picture display capacity by more than 25 per cent), doubling the reserve collection space and adding much needed offices and laboratories. The original plan was in fact far more ambitious than the final scheme, which left unbuilt a third of the extension the façade of which had been intended to stretch the entire length of Orange Street. George Pearce of the Ministry of Public Buildings and Works was in charge of the new extension, having inherited the work from his predecessors, Eric Bedford and W. Kendall.

The public architects had to tackle the not inconsiderable problem of adding a major extension to the north of Wilkins's building, and the result shows that they clearly had some stylistic struggles. They defined the northwest corner on Jubilee Walk with a careful copy of Wilkins's façade and on the main mass of the extension picked up the high Wilkins plinth, inventing a kind of abstract entablature in the projecting attic storey. The *Architects' Journal* at the time reported that the result was 'a worthy but timid design, debilitated by respect'. It further commented that 'If the extension keeps mutely in keeping with Wilkins in a formal sense, it fails more obviously in liveliness.' Sir John Summerson criticised the National Gallery (Wilkins) on the grounds that:

All the subsidiary sections have approximate equal value so that one is inclined to evaluate them as alternative suggestions rather than complementary parts of a single design. Be that as it may, the gallery is an interesting backcloth. The blank elevations of the extension show that the MPBW architects have not been able to find its equivalent in current forms of expression.

At about the same time the Tate Gallery was considering expansion and its architects were faced with the same problem of how to add onto a classical design in a way that respected the past and yet did not slavishly copy it. (One proposal was to stick a glass box across the main portico.) At the National Gallery caution prevailed and the architects failed either to invent a new language or to provoke any aesthetic thrill.

The 1970s were a curious period aesthetically. There was much concern expressed about simplifying the display of pictures and many a suspended ceiling and hessian panel were erected in the main galleries to conceal earlier architecture and decoration. At the same time, in 1977, the five-foot-high, lead-covered mansard was added to the front of the main building to conceal apparatus concerned with improving the atmospheric conditions of the galleries. This was done despite objections from conservation bodies and the Greater London Council – although proposals to change the main steps were not carried out. The architect Christopher Dean was commissioned by the Department of the Environment to remodel galleries 4 to 8 – rooms which then housed many of the Early Renaissance paintings now permanently installed in the Sainsbury Wing. Modern architectural fashion played a not inconsiderable part in the new displays. 'Undulating wall linings' provided recesses for altarpieces and russet-coloured carpet was chosen 'because of its similarity to red clay floor tiles of Italian churches of the period'. Some walls were painted turquoise because that was the complementary colour to the carpet. The three great paintings by Piero della Francesca were shown beneath new suspended ceilings.

While these relatively cosmetic changes were being made to the galleries during the 1970s, pressure was growing for the Government to make proper use of the Hampton site for the benefit of the National Gallery. The Chairman of the Trustees, Lord Annan, publicly stated that he had always hoped that the Government would consider the Hampton site as the natural choice for any extension to the National Gallery. During 1981 there was speculation in the press and, sensing a competition

The original design of the northern extension, produced in the late 1960s by the Ministry of Public Buildings and Works, was intended to stretch the entire length of Orange Street.

in the offing, *The Times* wrote in October of that year that private initiatives were going to be necessary because 'the era of public patronage, so strong since the last war, was over.'

In December 1981, the Secretary of State for the Environment, Michael Heseltine, announced a competition for the Hampton site. Heseltine had frequently spoken of his enthusiasm for competitions – at a *Financial Times* Industrial Architecture Award luncheon the previous year he had said: 'I would like to see more competitions for the design of new buildings. . . . I know that people are often sceptical about architectural competitions because of the risks associated with them – expense, delays, wild designs. But if the competition is properly run, the cost should be insignificant set beside the cost of the building. There need be no unacceptable delay.' Prophetic words indeed.

The competition that he announced for the new extension of the National Gallery was an unusual one. It was to select both an architect and a developer. The Government was prepared to grant a 125-year lease on the Hampton site in return for the provision by the developer of top-lit gallery space. Developers could fill the rest of the site with offices – the space they occupied reverting to the Government at the end of the lease. The Gallery Trustees proposed the idea of mixed development as the only feasible way of funding the building of the desperately needed new galleries.

'The winning scheme', the announcement said, 'will be selected on the basis of the architectural quality of the overall design and the quality and amount of space offered free of charge for use by the National Gallery.' Entrants were advised to consult the RIBA, Westminster City Council and the Royal Fine Art Commission – any planning application would be called in by Michael Heseltine and 'considered in the light of the recommendations of the competition advisers'. The advisers for the project were Lord Annan, Leonard Barr Smith, Sir Hugh Casson, W. D. Lacey, and the Director of the National Gallery, Sir Michael Levey, and it was they who were instructed to 'assess entries'. There was, however, an escape clause for the minister, which stated that 'if the Property Services Agency is unable or does not wish to proceed with the development, it will have no further commitment to the competition, or to proceed with the work.'

The brief for the entrants took two forms. A simple duplicated document for architects, and a glossy brochure detailing the virtues of the prime site for developers. In architectural terms the brief was basic, suggesting that the new building must relate in height, scale and finish to its neighbours. The gallery brief itself was thorough and asked for at least 20,000 square feet of gallery space for the Early Renaissance paintings – that is, in length, some 500 feet of wall space. The new galleries were to 'combine flexibility with a strong architectural character appropriate to the nation's prime collection of paintings . . . the character of the new exhibition space might be rather church or basilica like.' There was also an indication that finishes in the galleries should not be overassertive, and additional provision was also requested for a much needed audio-visual theatre, a coffee

shop and the usual space for warders, stores and lavatories.

By April 1982 there were 79 entrants for the first stage of the competition, of which seven were short-listed and asked to develop their designs.

Ahrends Burton and Koralek with Trafalgar House Developments Limited.

Arup Associates with Rosehaugh Company Limited.

Covell, Matthews, Wheatley with London and Edinburgh Investment Trust Company Limited.

Richard Rogers with Speyhawk plc.

Sheppard Robson with London and Metropolitan Estates.

Skidmore, Owings and Merrill with London Land Investments and Property Company Limited.

Spratley and Cullearn with Barratt Properties Limited.

THE 1982–4 GOVERNMENT COMPETITION

Opposite *Interior and exterior designs by Ahrends Burton and Koralek, and* (bottom) *Arup Associates' entry.*
Left *Richard Rogers's design in the style of his Pompidou Centre.*

The seven schemes were shown at the Gallery for two weeks from the end of August, an exhibition that was to prove something of a turning point for the whole competition. There was a large attendance and the press took up the subject of a new building in Trafalgar Square with enthusiasm. More than 78,000 people saw the display of architectural models in the Gallery and some 11,150 of them stated their preferences for both their favourite and least favourite schemes on questionnaires provided. Adopting a points system for a weighted score,

the public's first, second and third choices were, in the following order: Ahrends Burton and Koralek, Arup Associates, and Richard Rogers. The system adopted for the public voting created some anomalies, particularly in the case of Richard Rogers's scheme, which attracted 29 per cent of the first choice votes and 36 per cent of the 'least popular' votes – by far the largest number.

Richard Rogers, whose Lloyds of London building was under construction at the time of the National Gallery com-

petition, had produced a design in the style of his Paris Pompidou Centre. Inevitably, in the Portland stone environs of Trafalgar Square, it was seen as highly controversial. At a press preview of the exhibition of the designs the President of the RIBA, Owen Luder, made a memorable pronouncement about his reasons for preferring the Rogers scheme: 'I hope they choose that one, that is the work of a man who has said "That is what I think the answer is and sod you." The others have all been overawed by the site.' This set the architectural cats among the Trafalgar Square pigeons.

By the middle of September the competition advisers were expected to have made their final choice. Nothing was heard until 21 October, when they announced that they had had difficulty in choosing a clear winner and instead had decided to ask three firms of architects – Ahrends Burton and Koralak, Arup Associates and Skidmore, Owings and Merrill – to develop their proposals further, adding that 'in each case we believe that the building proposed should be modified.'

There were naturally some objections to this procedure, particularly from the short-listed architects whose work was not selected for further development. There was much talk in the architectural world of 'moving the goal posts' and one of the short-listed firms not selected for the third stage made it clear that they considered it 'completely unjust morally' to allow final, short-listed architects to alter designs, and alter them again until the assessors were happy.

There was great discontent about the way the well-intentioned competition was proceeding, and this must have been due to the difficulty for the competitors of pleasing two clients. The architects were in fact working for their developer partners and at the same time learning how to work for their official client, the National Gallery. The Gallery Director and Trustees naturally wanted to see the best possible galleries for some of the most valuable of the nation's paintings. But a whole new element (which should not have been unexpected)

had emerged during the exhibition of the short-listed designs: the vociferous public concern for the appearance of whatever was built in Trafalgar Square. There was also a debate within the profession about the style of the new building. That was to prove to be an area where there were no winners, but the ghosts of the architects of earlier National Gallery competitions must have stirred with some amusement in their respective gothic and classical tombs. The Gallery was constant in its one desire to provide an appropriate home for the paintings, but the debate had escalated and there is no doubt that public pressure played a part in the eventual outcome, especially as the press had entered into the debate with such relish. However, public opinion was mainly concerned with outside appearances – inside the Gallery it was the planning of the spaces for the pictures that concerned both staff and Trustees.

Between October and December 1982 there was much discussion and argument at the Gallery and in architects' offices. There was also debate in Whitehall, where the minister had reserved the final decision to himself after assessing the views of the advisers. The Gallery Trustees were unanimous in their preference for the proposals of Skidmore, Owings and Merrill and in particular for their gallery plan. At an evening meeting just before the announcement of the advisers' report, Lord Annan, Chairman of the Trustees, stressed to the minister that the Trustees wanted Skidmore, Owings and Merrill's scheme. The minister, however, had been advised that the Royal Fine Art Commission would not back this scheme and so insisted on the acceptance of the architects Ahrends Burton and Koralek with the developer Trafalgar House.

Lord Annan announced to the press, before the official report was released, that all the short-listed schemes had been rejected and that Ahrends Burton and Koralek with their developers, Trafalgar House, would be asked to produce a new design. He admitted that the choice was a compromise reached under pressure 'from the architectural establishment'. Sir Hugh Casson, one of the advisers, let it be known that the exterior of the Skidmore, Owings and Merrill building was unacceptable, and although he had earlier addressed the Trustees he had not been able to shift their loyalties from this scheme. The advisers, in fact, felt that they could not unanimously recommend any one of the schemes, but the minister wanted a winner and the only solution was to choose an architect and a developer to start from scratch. The National Gallery was therefore obliged to accept a result it was unhappy with; things did not bode well for the next phase.

Designs for the 1982 Government competition by Covell, Matthews, Wheatley (opposite); Skidmore, Owings and Merrill (left); Sheppard Robson (below); and Spratley and Cullearn (bottom).

The next phase was to be long and tiresome for all concerned. There was a need to produce an amended brief that suited all parties, especially the National Gallery. Obviously influenced by the SOM design, the Gallery made it clear that it favoured rooms with skirting boards, cornices and architraves. Slightly more controversially it had originally suggested that the character of the space for the pictures 'might be church or basilica like'. The use of the word 'basilica' was intended to suggest a centralised plan with lofty, dignified rooms that had a sense of ceremony and procession, as it was felt that the Early Renaissance paintings to be hung in the new wing would undoubtedly look at home in the kind of spaces characteristic of early Christian churches. The Gallery now explained that 'There is no need to create a pastiche of a 14th-century or 15th-century interior.' Instead it proposed 'an understated, rather bare modern idiom with colourless walls suggestive of stone. The galleries should have a sense of finished space, tranquillity and security. They should be substantial and im-

part an air of permanence. A sense of formality and balance appropriate to paintings of the Early Renaissance is needed. The character of the galleries should not dominate the paintings. . . . A rectilinear layout is required. The layout should provide a degree of ceremony appropriate to the profound experience of looking at paintings.' Lighting, it was emphasised, was to be *perceived* as daylight and an 'ideal hang'

was drawn up by the curatorial staff to explain the chronological and geographical groupings of the paintings.

In retrospect, to almost anyone involved in the problems of expanding the National Gallery, 1983 must now be seen as a disastrous year. Good intentions on so many sides came to nothing. At the end of 1982 Lord Annan had written to the Trustees airing his anxieties and asking the Building Committee (Trustee representatives were Bridget Riley, Lord Dufferin, Stuart Young and Lord Annan) to be sure that they were happy with the exterior appearance as well as with the interior working of any new design. He pointed out that the developers Trafalgar House were anxious not to waste time or money, and that while he felt the Trustees had no choice but to do all they could to help ABK submit satisfactory designs, 'we must face the possibility that we will not be satisfied.'

A great deal of work was done on the revised design by the architects, a Gallery working party and the Building Committee. Early in 1983 the working party visited Germany and Holland, by February the expanded design brief was approved, and in April the architects, represented by Peter Ahrends, presented their new scheme, which featured a glazed atrium and a tower on Trafalgar Square. The Building Committee gave their general approval, reported to the Board of Trustees and commenced consultations with the Royal Fine Art Commission. This was when some of the troubles began – the Secretary of the Royal Fine Art Commission made such extensive comments that the architects felt it necessary to modify the design. The subsequent revised scheme was then re-shown to the Building Committee, from which there was much criticism of the angular design of the tower topped by an array of masts. As late as July 1983 the Trustees were reluctant to approve the ABK design, despite the pressure they were under from Trafalgar House who were indicating that their relationship with the Gallery might be nearing its end if agreement on the major aspects of the design was not forthcoming. It did not help matters that the Royal Fine Art Commission disagreed with the National Gallery about the design of the galleries themselves, suggesting it would be more pleasant to rearrange the galleries so that there was 'space to escape' – for example, sitting areas with views of London. It was clear that the Commission, as a club mainly composed of architects, was determined to support the design.

Part of the reason for the prolonged design stage was that the architects selected by the developer had never designed an art gallery before. The major difficulty, however, seems to have been entrenched architectural attitudes and a confusion over which party was the client. The complicated formula that had brought together a property developer, the Government and the National Gallery was clearly not working. It is apparent from correspondence at the time that the architects felt that they were working for Trafalgar House and they had difficulty in accepting criticism from the Gallery on any area of the building that was not specifically to do with the hanging of pictures. Criticism of the tower and its idiosyncratic flagpoles was to return to haunt them after the public inquiry, but they were very reluctant to listen to others' views. It was not until December that Trafalgar House considered that they had sufficient agreement to apply for planning permission and listed building consent. The final design was released to the press with the Trustees taking the unusual step of simultaneously expressing their reservations. Press comment was almost uniformly unfavourable, as a consequence of which the Secretary of State for the Environment called in the application and a date was set for a public inquiry in April 1984.

There was opposition to the scheme from the Greater London Council's Historic Buildings Division, Westminster City Council, the Westminster Society, the London Society, the Georgian Group and a variety of individuals and third parties. It cannot be said, however, that the inquiry generated many fireworks or much public interest. Indeed, the Planning Inspector himself commented that 'a striking feature of the inquiry was the lack of involvement and attendance.' Following the public inquiry the Inspector's report was published in June 1984 and in one of those familiar aesthetico-legal judgments the Inspector agreed that the design for the new wing was not outstanding but nevertheless argued that it should be built. However, the Secretary of State for the Environment refused planning permission and listed building consent, as a result of which the Trustees and Trafalgar House decided to hang fire until early 1985.

Before this decision was taken there had been another, now famous, public pronouncement on the new extension. In May 1984 HRH The Prince of Wales had been invited to speak at a Royal Gala Evening to celebrate the 150th anniversary of the Royal Institute of British Architects, which was held at Hampton Court Palace. His Royal Highness did not deliver the expected congratulatory platitudes, however, and instead reminded architects of their duty to the public. Deploring the quality of much post-war British architecture, he specifically mentioned two London proposals that were worrying him and

many others. The first was Peter Palumbo's plan to demolish a listed section of the City of London by the Mansion House and to replace it with a tower by the late Mies van der Rohe – a building that the Prince called 'a glass stump more suited to downtown Chicago than the City of London.' The second was the National Gallery extension over which so many tears had already been shed. This design, too, failed to get off lightly. Expressing his concern over what had happened to the capital since the bomb damage of the Second World War, the Prince demanded:

> What are we shortly going to do to one of its most famous areas – Trafalgar Square? Instead of designing an extension to the elegant façade of the National Gallery which complements it and continues the concept of columns and domes, it looks as though we may be presented with a kind of vast municipal fire station, complete with the sort of tower that contains the siren. I would understand this type of High Tech approach if you demolished the whole of Trafalgar Square and started again with a single architect responsible for the entire layout, but what is proposed is like a monstrous carbuncle on the face of a much loved and elegant friend. Apart from anything else, it defeats me why anyone wishing to display the Early Renaissance pictures belonging to the Gallery should do so in a new gallery so manifestly at odds with the whole spirit of that age of astonishing proportion.

The architects of the new extension, as prominent figures of the RIBA establishment, were among the stunned audience who heard this early essay in royal architectural criticism which was to have such a profound effect.

Clearly the Gallery needed help to resolve the dilemma in which it found itself. But the help would have to be of the kind that could provide an extension for the Early Renaissance paintings without the obligation to fund it by commercial development on the same site. The nub of the problem had been the unhappy mixture of uses, and what had been proposed as a solution in fact resulted in a sad and ugly stalemate: an unhappy marriage had produced a rejected progeny. A well-intentioned but misguided scheme had gone badly wrong, and during the last months of 1984 the Board of Trustees decided to examine ways of finding private sponsorship for a new building that could be entirely dedicated to the National Gallery's use.

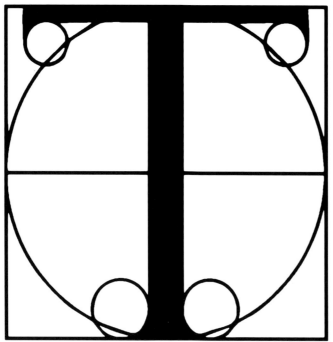

CHAPTER 3

HE SEARCH FOR AN ARCHITECT

A miracle did happen. When the Board of Trustees met on 26 March 1985 they were told of an amazing and unexpected gift. The public announcement was made at noon on 2 April 1985, when the Trustees revealed that they had received 'the most remarkable and munificent gift'. Three brothers – John, Simon, and Timothy Sainsbury – had expressed their wish to give to the nation a new building on the Hampton site for the exclusive use of the National Gallery.

This extraordinary donation was to provide the growing number of visitors to the National Gallery with new, improved facilities for lectures and temporary exhibitions as well as more top-lit galleries and a new shop and restaurant. Wary of the whole delicate question of the choice of architect, the donors emphasised that this was a decision to be made jointly by the donors and the Trustees, aided by a selection committee. At a press conference attended by the donors, the Chairman of the Trustees explained that it was their intention, with the assistance of expert advice, to invite up to six architects from an international list to submit their design approaches, from which short list one architect would be chosen. It was also made clear that any new building would have to relate sympathetically to the old building, have an architectural distinction worthy of the site and be complementary to Trafalgar square. This attitude had moved a long way from the Trustees' former reluctant approval of a design that they were unhappy with and that had not, in their view, added distinction to the square. The acceptance of the magnificent gift gave the Gallery a joint responsibility with the Sainsbury brothers to ensure that any resulting new set of galleries was of the highest possible quality.

The selection of the right architect was obviously crucial, there were many parties to please and the whole question of what was to be built on the Hampton site had become a public cause célèbre. To ensure that the best architect was chosen enormously elaborate procedures were followed. A great deal was learnt from the experience of the J. Paul Getty Trust in America, which had recently pursued a lengthy search for an

architect for its new museum in Los Angeles. It was the Getty Trustees who had devised the idea of a selection committee, ruling out both private selection by the donors as well as any form of open architectural competition.

The selection committee set up by the National Gallery consisted of the three donors, Sir John Sainsbury, The Hon. Simon Sainsbury and The Hon. Timothy Sainsbury MP, and, from the National Gallery, Sir Michael Levey (Director), Allan Braham (Keeper) and Michael Wilson (Deputy Keeper).

The Trustees of the Gallery were represented by the Chairman (Lord Annan until June 1985, when he was succeeded by The Hon. Jacob Rothschild), Lord Dufferin, Caryl Hubbard, Bridget Riley and Stuart Young. They invited Sir Isaiah Berlin, a former Trustee whose advice they particularly valued, to join them. An adviser on the construction of the new building was appointed, property developer Stuart Lipton.

At their first meeting the committee decided to appoint two consultants who had specialist knowledge of contemporary architecture, Ada Louise Huxtable, the distinguished former architectural correspondent of the *New York Times* and a member of the selection committee of the J. Paul Getty Museum, and Colin Amery, the architectural correspondent of the *Financial Times* in London. They were to become known as the official 'hand-holders'.

The process of consultation that followed was lengthy and wide ranging. There were three main approaches: research carried out by Michael Wilson for the Gallery and Grizelda Grimond for the Trustees; advice sought from a broad spec-

The donors of the new wing: from the left, Simon, John, and Timothy Sainsbury.

51

trum of architects and architectural authorities; and discussions, interviews and presentations with many of the architects themselves. This three-pronged approach was intended to ensure that both the Gallery and the Trustees were as informed as possible before making their selection. In addition to the extensive interviews and discussions, an important aspect of the research was the programme of visits made to new museum and gallery buildings throughout the world.

There were undoubtedly some advantages to be gained from the long delays inflicted upon the development of the Hampton site. The 1970s and 1980s were a period of remarkable growth for museums and galleries worldwide. There was scarcely one well-known architect who had not designed a new museum or an extension to an existing one. The museum was one building type that offered architects the opportunity of presenting their work on a truly public stage, for museums were places constantly full of 'the public'. The American architect Philip Johnson had an explanation for the enthusiasm that the architect feels for new museums and galleries: 'Purely aesthetically speaking, the museum is an architect's dream He has as in a church – to make the visitor happy, to put him in a receptive frame of mind while he is undergoing an emotional experience. We architects welcome the challenge.'

The new museum building had become, during this period, more than just a stepping stone in the pathway of contemporary architecture – it was a symbol of local or national cultural growth. The United Kingdom, however, remaining true to its history, was comparatively late in the development of its museums. The nineteenth century was a

period of rapid growth (similar to that which has been seen this century in the United States), but in the twentieth century things moved more slowly. In 1972 the City of London provided a completely new home for the Museum of London in the Barbican (architects Powell and Moya), and in 1983 the city of Glasgow opened a museum for the Burrell Collection (architect Barry Gasson). Two branches of one family, the Sainsburys, have contributed both the new wing for the National Gallery and the Sainsbury Centre for Visual Arts at the University of East Anglia. The Clore Gallery (architect James Stirling) at the Tate Gallery in London, built for the collection bequeathed to the nation by J. M. W. Turner, is the other outstanding gift by a private donor.

The exceptional wealth of new museums abroad was to make 'the search' for an architect for the Sainsbury Wing into an interesting and fruitful perambulation around the world for the selection committee. In Europe the travels began in Denmark to see the much praised Louisiana Museum, which houses the collection of Knud Jensen. Begun in the 1950s, and run as a foundation, it is often seen as the model museum for a democratic society. It is situated at Humlebæk, a small wooded country estate outside Copenhagen, on the shores of a beautiful lake. An original 1850s house forms the heart of the museum, but the galleries and exhibition space (designed by architects Jorgen Bo and Vilhelm Wohlert) stretch away from the house into the woods and down to the lake. The architects adopted the style of Mies van der Rohe, but softened it by the use of timber and tile. Knud Jensen founded his museum as a conscious reaction to the conventional museums of the nineteenth century, which he feels 'were built in one of the architectural dark ages, in the ambitious bourgeois style of the last century with masses of columns and marble staircases – pompous and mindless prestige architecture.' Seeing the Louisiana buildings with their more relaxed and informal approach was helpful because it showed a completely different kind of relationship between the public and the exhibited art works from that encouraged by earlier museums. Older museums provide lessons and inspiration of a different kind, and in Copenhagen, by way of contrast to Louisiana, the Carlsberg Glyptotek and the Thorvaldsens Museum were both visited by members of the committee.

It was Paris that was perhaps most likely to provide useful examples of the expansion of nineteenth-century galleries in the centre of a city. The Pompidou Centre (one of the great cultural monuments of the 1970s, celebrating a particular moment of technological euphoria) was instructive in showing both the strengths and weaknesses of a high-tech approach to the architecture of public buildings. Renzo Piano and Richard Rogers's creation has been popular with the public, but it has often proved to be far from ideal for the exhibition of works of art. For this reason the National Gallery team were keen to see the work of the Italian architect Gae Aulenti, who in the mid-1980s had been commissioned to redesign parts of the interior. These alterations, while demonstrating the building's flexibility, also show that certain kinds of works of art demand certain kinds of settings. In the jagged high-tech environment Aulenti has installed a series of homogenous and orthodox rooms that are highly successful for the display of paintings. Her experience gained in the conversion of the Musée d'Orsay and in the refurbishment of the Palazzo Grassi in Venice provided helpful lessons for any prospective architectural jury concerned with the commissioning of a new gallery.

Also on the itinerary was Roland Simounet's adaptation of the Hôtel Salé for the new Musée Picasso – one of the most interesting and successful displays of modern art within the context of an old building. It had some lessons for the National Gallery – these were concerned with an examination of the reasons why it created such a successful ambience for the enjoyment of Picasso's paintings.

Germany is surely the country of the new museum. After the explosion of new centres for the performing arts during the 1950s and 1960s, museum and gallery building took place on a scale that is staggering to anyone in Britain used to the parsimonious struggles necessary to achieve the least advance. Three museums were of particular interest to the committee: the Neue Staatsgalerie in Stuttgart, designed by the British architect James Stirling; the Museum für Kunsthandwerk, Frankfurt, by the American architect Richard Meier; and the Städtisches Museum at Mönchengladbach, designed by the Viennese Hans Hollein. There was particular relevance in visiting the Staatsgalerie in Stuttgart for as well as being an addition to a nineteenth-century classical building it was an opportunity to inspect an important work by the much admired architect, James Stirling. Stirling was likely to feature on any short list of architects because of his highly original designs, as well as for his considerable experience in the art gallery field: in 1978 James Stirling, Michael Wilford and Associates were appointed architects to the Tate Gallery and asked to draw up a long-term master plan, of which the first

Left *The Pompidou Centre in Paris is an icon of the 'high-tech' school of architecture and is popular as a great piece of engineering offering views of Paris – rather like the Eiffel Tower. Although a crowd-puller, it has not weathered well.*
Below *The Staatsgalerie in Stuttgart was extended by the British architect James Stirling in a manner that is full of historical references and engaging architectural jokes. The new building is as much an exhibit as anything shown inside it.*

Despite some of the vagaries of the exterior of the Clore Gallery at the Tate, London, James Stirling's galleries for the paintings of the Turner Bequest are conventional. Their form is a response to the need for daylight, which is filtered from above.

phase, the Clore Gallery, built to house the Turner Collection, was opened in 1987. Stirling had also produced interesting entries for new museum competitions in Cologne and Düsseldorf, and the committee were later to visit his Sackler Museum at the Fogg Art Museum at Harvard University.

The extension to the Staatsgalerie is one of the most evocative and powerful new buildings in Europe. It occupies a generous site which appears on plan to be larger than that of the old museum, and it deals admirably with the difficult problem of relating to an existing neo-classical building. In itself the extension is decidedly monumental and clearly inspired by the work of Boullée, Weinbrenner and Schinkel. The formally planned galleries are top-lit by glazed lay lights (flat glass ceilings which filter daylight and provide additional artificial lighting from behind), which are suitable for both traditional and modern art. The public spaces enjoy the light from a dazzling serpentine window, and there is a great open drum at the centre of the museum which provides a place for sitting in the sun and a public route through the building. The Staatsgalerie has enjoyed a huge increase in visitors since the addition of the new wing, and there is no doubt that it is admired as much for its new architecture as for its collections.

Hans Hollein's museum at Mönchengladbach, completed in 1985, was visited as a representative example of the work of an architect renowned for his flair in the display of art, and for the sense of glamour in his work. This museum – one of several he has completed – is purposefully designed to be an important feature in the town, and the breaking up into separate elements of the various functions associated with the museum gives the building something of the atmosphere of a small village community.

Then on to Frankfurt, where, along the river, there is an array of new museums that is in many ways a representative exhibition of modern museum architecture. It is a remarkable collection, particularly the work of the American architect Richard Meier at the Museum für Kunsthandwerk, also completed in 1985. Meier has become one of the leading architects in the world of museum design, not least because of his success in winning the invited competition to design one of the major museums of the twentieth century, the new J. Paul Getty Museum in Los Angeles. His Frankfurt projects and the High Museum of Art in Atlanta, Georgia, have been particularly influential. Meier has said that his rather neutral modern architecture – once known as 'white' architecture – is ideal for encouraging the rediscovery of aesthetic values and for conveying that sense of the museum as a place of contemplation. He is also convinced that any new museum building should encourage the appreciation of the art of architecture.

The committee also visited the Alte Pinakothek, Munich (architect Leo von Klenze, 1826–36, rebuilt by Hans Dollgast, 1952–7); the Glyptothek, Munich (Leo von Klenze, 1816–34, rebuilt by Joseph Weiderman, 1967–72); and the Neue Pinakothek, Munich (Alexander Freiherr von Branca, 1974–81). The great modern staircase in the Alte Pinakothek was a memorable example of the need for spaces that instill in the visitor a mood of disinterested contemplation as he approaches the works of art.

America and her new art museums have had an enormous influence upon developments in Europe. It was therefore natural that the selection committee should wish to make an extensive tour of that country. The United States has long been the land of the generous private donor – there is there a unique sense of private obligation to the public realm that has not been felt in Britain since the nineteenth century. The combination of some remarkable private collections and a positive wish to make them accessible to the public has bred in the twentieth century a major crop of new museum buildings. Largely purpose-built, American museums set high environmental standards; they are highly unlikely to be converted palaces and are therefore easily able to provide a wide range of public facilities to accompany the collection. It is commonplace to find lecture rooms and education facilities alongside the growing commercial areas of shops and restaurants. The Metropolitan Museum of Art in New York, for example, has always felt like some great cultural liner moored on Fifth Avenue, with every desirable facility on board.

It should be said here, that once the decision had been made to build on the whole of the Hampton site in London, it had always been the intention of the Sainsbury brothers to improve the public facilities for education as well as to provide new galleries. Speaking in 1986 to the National Art Collections Fund, the Chairman of the Trustees, The Hon. Jacob Rothschild (now Lord Rothschild), made clear what he felt the public demanded from modern museums and what they should expect on the Hampton site:

> We now have not only the opportunity to create galleries for Early Renaissance paintings but also to put up a building which will contain those facilities which the public now expect from museums: temporary exhibition space, a lecture theatre and cinema, an information room, a gallery shop, a restaurant and generous public spaces.

The selection committee's visit to the United States took place in September 1985. The party on this occasion consisted of the donors, Jacob Rothschild, Lord Dufferin, Bridget Riley, Caryl Hubbard, Allan Braham, Ada Louise Huxtable and Colin Amery. It was their brief to look at a carefully selected range of new buildings and to meet architects and museum directors who had undergone the process of either commissioning a new museum or of adding new elements to an existing one.

The interviews began in New York with a meeting at the Madison Avenue offices of I. M. Pei Partnership. The practice is well known for its large number of public buildings, including the East Wing of the National Gallery of Art, Washington, DC (opened in June 1978), alterations at the Louvre, and additions to both the Portland Museum in Maine and Boston Museum of Fine Arts. The Charles Shipman Payson Building at Portland, completed in May 1983 and designed by Henry Cobb, a partner of I. M. Pei, was the building that particularly interested the committee. This was partly because it was the newest, but also because it houses Old Master paintings and had been highly recommended for the quality of natural light in its galleries, which had been achieved by lighting consultants Jules Fisher and Paul Marantz Inc.

It was seeing the buildings, however, rather than simply meeting the architects, that proved particularly helpful to the committee. At the Charles Shipman Payson Building two elements seemed relevant to the National Gallery's dilemma. One was the fact that, although in a small town, the Portland

extension had a job to do as a form of *architecture parlante* in a square. Cobb had also solved the problem of top lighting by means of a series of domed clerestories. From Portland's elegant brickwork the committee looked at the more orthodox galleries – also by I. M. Pei and Partners – at Boston Museum of Fine Arts. Here, Pei's West Wing (1977–81) has an arched galleria for sitting out and the actual gallery space forms a relatively small part of the new building. In the smoothness of its finish the Wing sits easily alongside the neo-Greek of the original museum.

At Cambridge, Massachusetts, the committee visited James Stirling's addition to the Fogg Art Museum at Harvard University, the Arthur M. Sackler Museum, named after its principal donor. When asked during the selection process, 'which is your favourite museum?', the answer given by the firm of James Stirling, Michael Wilford and Associates was Sir

Top *The architect of the extension to the Fogg Museum at Harvard, James Stirling, used the imagery of an Egyptian tomb entrance to suggest the hoard of treasures within.*
Above *A gallery designed by Louis Kahn for the Yale Center for British Art has a domestic feel – there is top light but also windows that look onto the outside world.*
Above right *Things are big in Texas: at the Dallas Museum of Art the arched central hall is a dignified centre to a museum that covers almost a whole city block.*

John Soane's Dulwich Picture Gallery (1811–14). This reply was considered by the Fogg selection committee to be highly sympathetic because it reinforced their desire to find a designer who could understand the domestic scale of the Fogg and the need for it to be used as a teaching museum rather than as a place for grand display. The result was an idiosyncratic building, whose unusual, informal monumentality Soane would have appreciated. The strong character of the building and its carefully designed individual rooms seemed a welcome break from the free-flowing and 'flexible' spaces of many of the newer museums.

Before leaving Cambridge some of the group interviewed the distinguished Spanish architect Rafael Moneo who was teaching at Harvard. His museum of antiquities at Merida had greatly impressed some of the Trustees.

The Yale Center for British Art was familiar to many of the party and is a much revered example of the work of the late American architect Louis Kahn. (After his death on 17 March 1974, the completion of the building was supervised by the architects Pellacchia and Meyers.) The Center was Kahn's last work, and alongside his Kimbell Art Museum in Fort Worth, Texas, has an almost iconic status. As a public museum and research institute devoted to British culture it offered many lessons to the British visitors. There was an enjoyable irony, too, in the sight of a visiting delegation from the old country's national collection visiting the New World to see the fine quality of the display conditions given to venerable works from its own shores.

Louis Kahn had taught at Yale and had designed the University Art Gallery in the 1950s. He was chosen as the natural candidate for being 'sensitive to both the world of art and the external world of everyday existence . . . a friend of daylight . . . [who] knows the visual refreshment afforded by views of the real world and by spatial variety.'

Dallas offered the chance to view the huge, newly opened Dallas Museum of Art (architect Edward Larrabee Barnes Associates). The museum is spread over a large downtown site and has at its centre a high vaulted hall. It is organised around a series of courtyards and has a long, gently cascading stairway that links the different areas of the museum. This Texan museum showed the visiting group the value of extremely up-to-date warding and security services, as well as a particularly high level of finish and materials.

Fort Worth is Dallas's neighbour and home of what many consider to be one of the finest examples of twentieth-century American architecture – Kahn's Kimbell Art Museum. This museum opened in 1972 and was the last work completed under the architect's own supervision. Kahn had always been preoccupied with the role of light in architecture, and at the Kimbell his cycloidal concrete vaults with narrow skylights and aluminium reflectors appear to diffuse the natural light effortlessly into the galleries. Great architecture is largely a matter of the skilful articulation of space and light, an understanding of materials and a sense of proportion. To find all these aspects combined in one building is rare, but they do coexist at the Kimbell. They do so in a fashion that is timeless. None of the visiting party had any doubt about this museum's architectural quality or about its rare and contemplative atmosphere.

Kahn came from Philadelphia, where he had many collaborators and students. His teachings led many to question the prevalent architectural dogma and to look at contemporary architecture in a new way. The young architect Robert Venturi worked with Kahn in the 1950s and the two shared similar ideas on spatial complexity and the 'layering' of buildings. The National Gallery committee thought it right to look for an architect who understood these changes in architectural thought, and who had worked with the one Western architect who seemed to have resolved so many of the contradictions inherent in designing public buildings for the modern world.

It was decided to return to New York to interview Robert Venturi and his partner Denise Scott Brown before going back to England. The subsequent discussion was based on these

architects' earlier submission of a 'statement of qualifications' and on the designs they were doing for the Seattle Art Museum and the Laguna Gloria Museum in Austin, Texas. From this meeting emerged many ideas about the special nature of the Gallery's needs, and the architects made it clear that they were interested not just in 'light focussing on art' but in designing a place of character. They also explained why they were averse to the idea of limited competitions, favouring instead intense collaboration between client and selected architect. However, all architects have at some time or another to bend their own rules, and Venturi and Scott Brown were prepared to go through the selection process for the prize of designing a new building for the National Gallery on Trafalgar Square.

In parallel to the extensive foreign travels an intensive search was also being carried out in Britain. By June 1985 the researchers and hand-holders had prepared a list of some 50 architects – the majority of these were British although several foreign firms were also included. A display of their work was arranged for the selection committee to look at in the National Gallery. Throughout the selection process consultations were held with a wide variety of architects and authorities on contemporary architecture in Britain and abroad. Among those consulted were Sir Denys Lasdun, Professor Colin St John Wilson, William Whitfield, Michael Manser (President of the Royal Institute of British Architects), members of the Royal Fine Art Commission and its Secretary Sherban Cantacuzino, Alvin Boyarsky (Chairman of the Architectural Association), Pontus Hulten from the Palazzo Grassi in Venice, S. Dillon Ripley (Secretary Emeritus of the Smithsonian), Charles Jencks and Philip Johnson (architect and Chairman of the Architectural Committee of the Board of Trustees of the Metropolitan Museum in New York).

Visits were also paid to the major new museums and galleries in this country, including the Burrell Collection in Glasgow (architect Barry Gasson); the Clore Gallery at the Tate, then under construction (architect James Stirling); extensions to the Whitechapel Art Gallery (architects Colquhoun and Miller); the Sainsbury Centre for Visual Arts at the University of East Anglia (architect Norman Foster); and the Museum of London (architects Powell and Moya). To complement these visits several architectural practices were also visited, as well as a variety of new buildings and architectural exhibitions. After the committee had considered the specially arranged exhibition of photographs and brochures of the work of some 50 practices, a preliminary short list was prepared.

Top *The Kimbell Art Museum in Fort Worth, designed by Louis Kahn, is widely considered to be the finest museum building of the late twentieth century.* Above *It is the play of light on pictures and marble surfaces that enchants the visitor to the Kimbell – the architect achieved a unique serenity in the galleries.* Left *The interior of the Sainsbury Centre (architect Sir Norman Foster) at the University of East Anglia at Norwich adopts a kind of universal space for an idiosyncratic collection.*

In England, old galleries have been successfully adapted and updated – the Whitechapel Art Gallery was completely revamped by architects Colquhoun and Miller.

However, the committee felt that having looked at the work of a great many international and British architectural 'stars', more smaller and younger British practices should be considered. Among these were several that represented the catholic spread of architectural ideas that are prevalent in Britain.

Julian Bicknell, who had recently designed a new Palladian villa in Cheshire and completed some work at Castle Howard, represented the younger converts to classicism. Piers Gough of the practice Campbell, Zogolovitch, Wilkinson and Gough is an architect who is harder to classify in stylistic terms. Although sometimes considered a post-modernist, as the designer of a successful Arts Council exhibition on the work of Sir Edwin Lutyens, at the Hayward Gallery in 1981–2, he showed a great understanding of the diversity of Lutyens's skills and the richness of the English architectural tradition. His housing schemes in East London and some of his Docklands proposals were examined by the committee.

Leon Krier is perhaps better known as a radical architectural theorist. His presentation to the committee suggested that the existing National Gallery was too large and the policy of ever expanding museums was a mistaken one. He produced some fine drawings of his ideas, which included a series of new classical pavilions in Trafalgar Square, designed to improve the townscape and break down the scale of the Gallery.

Jeremy Dixon was selected for initial interview on the strength of his firm's collaboration with the Building Design Partnership (Jeremy Dixon/BDP) on the development of the Royal Opera House in Covent Garden. His particular skills lie in his acute and thorough analysis of sites and his ability to design sensitive schemes that remain in keeping with their surroundings. His housing schemes in Maida Vale and North Kensington were visited.

John Outram represented a more strongly individual

architectural style – some of the committee visited the country house he had designed in a Sussex deer park, where he demonstrated a talent for architectural decoration and an unusual ability to use a rich palette of materials. The pumping station he designed on the Isle of Dogs is one of the more striking new buildings in the capital and represents a new sort of toughly detailed modern classicism.

A visit to the newly expanded Whitechapel Art Gallery gave the committee the opportunity to see the work of Alan Colquhoun and John Miller, who had faced, on a smaller scale, the problem of adding new galleries and public spaces onto an old building. This they had achieved very effectively in a modern style that harmonised with the original galleries.

Other architects who were seen or whose work was visited included Richard Reid, winner of the Epping Town Hall competition; Trevor Horne, who had designed a winning competition entry for the Oriental Museum at Durham University; Nicholas Hare, the runner-up in the Paris Opera competition; Nicholas Lacey, whose winning Crown Reach housing scheme had been built on London's Millbank by the Crown Estate; and Richard MacCormac, architect of the Sainsbury Building at Worcester College, Oxford.

By 4 October 1985, with what the records describe as 'a surprising amount of unanimity', the final short list was drawn up. The six invited to put forward proposals for the extension of the National Gallery on the Hampton site were:

Henry Nichols Cobb of I. M. Pei Partnership, USA
Colquhoun and Miller
Jeremy Dixon/BDP
Piers Gough of Campbell, Zogolovitch, Wilkinson and Gough
James Stirling, Michael Wilford and Associates
Venturi, Rauch and Scott Brown (USA)

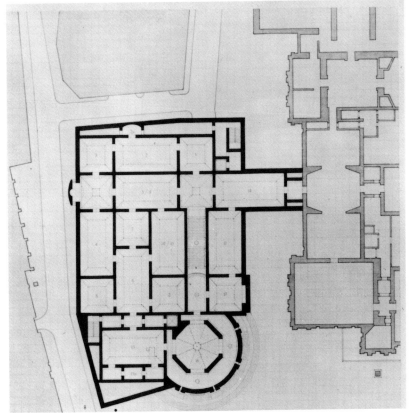

THE SHORT LIST OF ARCHITECTS *In October 1985 six architects were invited to put forward proposals for the National Gallery extension. Harry Cobb's design* (above) *followed a classical course with a rotunda at the knuckle of the scheme on Trafalgar Square. Gallery floor plan* (left).

Colquhoun and Miller's scheme was very understated and took the form of a stripped-down version of a Pall Mall clubhouse. Gallery floor plan (right).

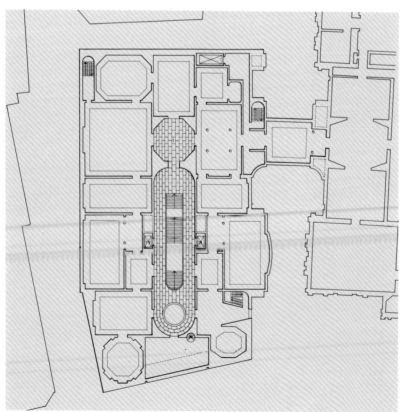

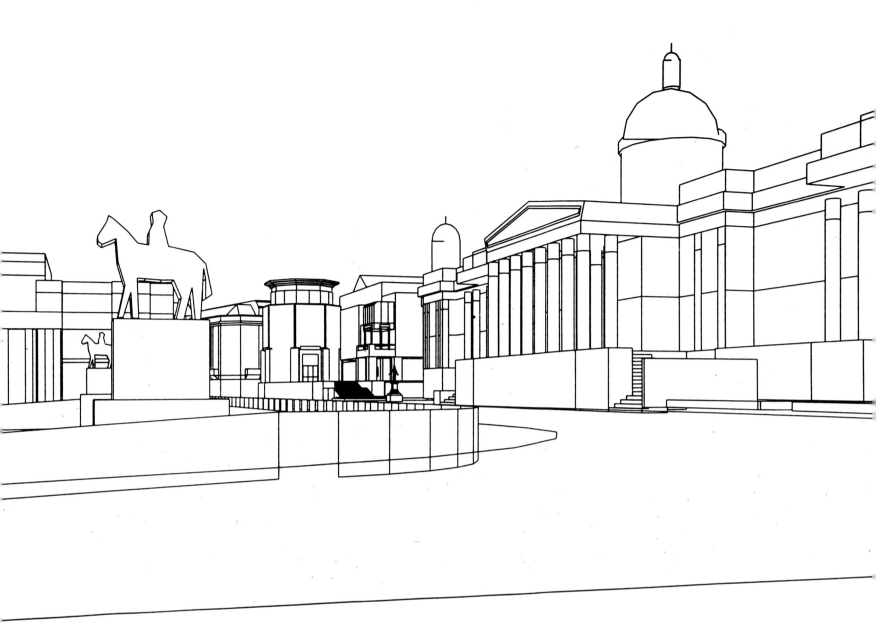

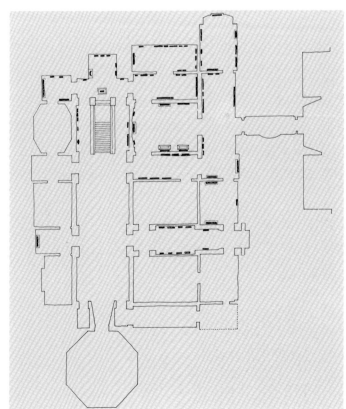

Jeremy Dixon's design featured an Italianate baptistery at the key point on the square, suggesting the spirit of the paintings within. Gallery floor plan (left).

Piers Gough gave great height to his scheme to complement the opposing tower of St Martin-in-the-Fields. His interiors included galleries with rich gold ceilings. Gallery floor plan (right).

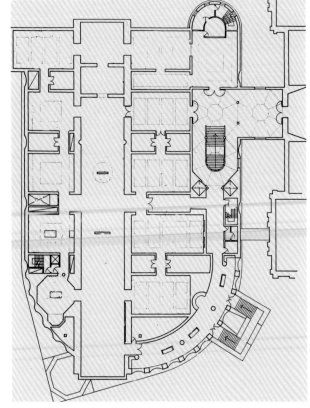

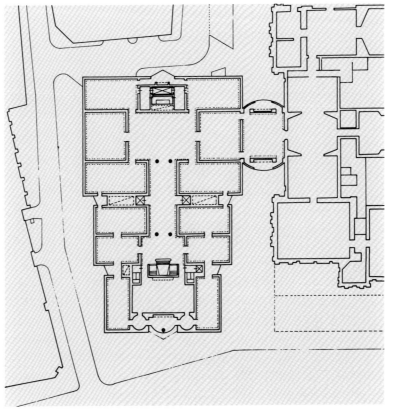

James Stirling, Michael Wilford and Associates designed a strong temple-like form that had many of Stirling's hallmarks. It was intricately planned with galleries apparently carved out of a solid form. Gallery floor plan (left).

Robert Venturi's scheme (above) *combined appropriateness with a subtle understanding of the National Gallery's neighbours and of London's scenography. Gallery floor plan* (right).
Opposite *View of Venturi's proposed extension from the porch of the National Gallery.*

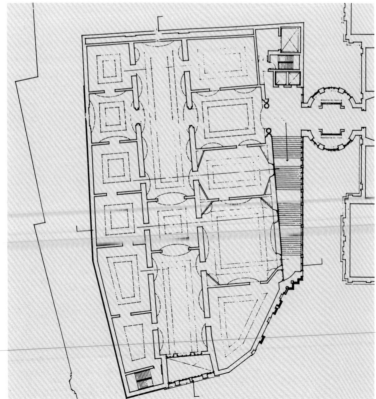

In mid-October the architects were sent a set of guidelines giving a provisional indication of the Gallery's requirements and designed 'to stimulate thoughts'. The intention was to enter into a full dialogue with the selected architect and to prepare, with him, the comprehensive brief.

The momentum continued with the short list being made public. The architects were given until the middle of January 1986 to prepare for their presentations and interviews. The guidelines made it clear that everyone concerned with the project was determined to achieve 'a building of outstanding architectural distinction to complete the historic square', while also emphasising that what was needed was a sympathetic neighbour for the Wilkins building and a set of galleries 'of a quality and character appropriate to the paintings'.

The results of this selection process were both varied and fascinating. The selection committee met over a three-day weekend at the National Gallery to judge the finalists' submissions. Drawings and models had been displayed in the board room for a period before the judging. Each architectural team discussed its submission at length, after which a technical assessment of each entry was made and presented to the selection board by the consultants and advisers. At the end of three days of interviews the committee was unanimous in its selection of Venturi, Rauch and Scott Brown from Philadelphia. Before the result was made public several of the committee members made a further visit to the United States to see the architects' offices and to meet some of their previous clients, most notably at Princeton University.

Towards the end of January a press conference was held at the National Gallery to announce the result of the competition. The Chairman of the Trustees reminded his audience of the tireless work of the selection committee – as he said, 'the hunting of architects knows no closed season.' He also stressed that throughout the selection process the committee was looking not so much for a finished building design but for an architect. Following the selection of the architect there was to be a period in which architect and client worked together on the development of the brief and the scheme. The final design would not be revealed to the public until April 1987.

Venturi, who told the press that they were looking at 'the happiest architect in the world', also gave a gentle hint of the look of his proposals: 'Our goal has been to create a building positive in its architectural quality – and yet sensitive to the rest of Trafalgar Square and appropriate as a context itself for the masterpieces within it.'

CHAPTER 4

OBERT VENTURI AND HIS DESIGN

To anyone who had known Venturi well over the years his appointment seemed entirely appropriate. He was one of a very small band of architects who was reluctant to break completely with the past as a source of inspiration, who was eclectic and hard to pin down in his choice of architectural styles and who had long appreciated both English and Italian architecture. In the press conference following his selection he outlined his plans for the Sainsbury Wing:

> We will work for a building that will grow out of its context, that of this William Wilkins fabric and the square itself – take off from what's here and at the same time, and in the end, enhance what's here. Our approach will be to create harmony within the whole by combining contrast and analogy, that is, some elements in the new building that are contrasting with, and others that are analogous to, those of the old building. We intend to maintain for instance, the height-line of the existing building, match its Portland stone and extend and take off from the matchless rhythmic quality of its historic façade. At the same time we will combine and unify other elements which will contrast with those next door so that this new work will be a confident and worthy contemporary work.

Venturi was born in 1925 in Philadelphia and trained at Princeton University School of Architecture. As the winner of the Rome Prize (a leading prize for American architectural students that enables the winner to study at the American Academy in Rome), he spent two formative years in Italy (1954–6). In the early days of his career he worked for Eero Saarinen and Louis Kahn and taught at the universities of Pennsylvania and Yale. He formed a partnership with John Rauch in 1964, which his wife, Denise Scott Brown, joined in 1967. (Rauch left the partnership in 1989.)

Venturi issued what he called his 'gentle manifesto' in 1966 when he published his book *Complexity and Contradiction in Architecture*, described by Professor Vincent Scully in

his introduction as 'the most important book on the making of architecture since Le Corbusier's *Vers une Architecture* of 1923.' In this controversial book Venturi made a relatively simple plea for architecture to be richer and more allusive, and argued for a more vital architecture that derived its validity from diversity and depth of meaning. He examined, too, the work of several English architects, and was one of the very first architects to appreciate the importance of the work of Sir Edwin Lutyens.

As a subtle theorist Venturi seemed to be the right man for the job. He had proved himself able to work in both a contextual and a scenographic way that augured well for the difficult Trafalgar Square site. The firm was also working concurrently on three other museum buildings: the Seattle Art Museum in downtown Seattle, Washington; the Laguna Gloria Museum in Austin, Texas; and the Contemporary Art Museum at La Jolla, California. The firm had added a wing to the Allen Memorial Art Museum for Oberlin College, Ohio, in 1973, and much earlier had been responsible for improvements to the Duke mansion for the Institute of Fine Arts in New York.

One of the many recommendations that the Trustees of the National Gallery received concerning the work of Venturi, Rauch and Scott Brown was an interesting letter from the Special Advisor to the Minister of Communications of the Government of Canada, Jean Sutherland Boggs, who had been asked to give up her post as Director of the Philadelphia Museum of Art to head a special Crown Corporation to recommend sites and architects for and to supervise the design and building of both the new National Gallery of Canada and the National Museum of Man. She had earlier appointed Venturi as architect to the Philadelphia Museum of Art, where his task was to make a master plan for the improved use of the 1920s Beaux-Arts building. She praised Venturi's understanding of the nature of an old building and his ability to make an extension that was both sympathetic and original.

As part of the process of working through his brief and discovering as much as possible about how the National Gallery viewed its Early Renaissance collection – and in particular the remarkable assembly of early Italian paintings – it was decided that a visit to Italy for the architects and members of the 'client group' would be helpful. It was hoped that seeing Italian art both in museums and in the settings for which it was originally painted would be enlightening for all concerned with the project. It was also part of the essential process of architect and client getting to know each other. As Venturi

VENTURI'S PUBLIC BUILDINGS

Right *Renovation and addition to the Allen Memorial Art Museum, Oberlin College, Ohio, 1973–6 – a large wing added to Cass Gilbert's museum and harmonised by the use of materials.*
Far right *Competition design for the State Mosque in Baghdad, 1983, where Venturi's facility for pattern-making fortuitously coincided with the Islamic understanding of geometric ornament. This design was not built.*

Above *The Molecular Biology Building at Princeton University, Princeton, New Jersey, 1983–5. The patterned brickwork and use of natural oak inside the building humanises a laboratory block.*
Right *Model of the Seattle Art Museum in Washington State. Opened in 1991.*

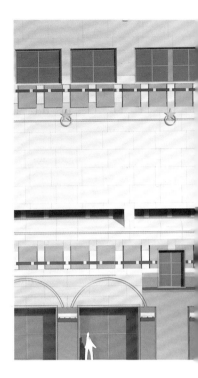

Top *Gordon Wu Hall at Princeton University, Princeton, New Jersey, 1983. The staircase is undoubtedly in the spirit of the work of Lutyens – it acts as a gathering place and amphitheatre for student meetings.*
Left *The exterior planning of Gordon Wu Hall eases the building into the Neo-Gothic campus. This view shows Venturi's sundial.*
Above *Project (unbuilt) for the Laguna Gloria Museum, Austin, Texas, 1984.*

Right *The house as a
simplified form – the Vanna
Venturi house in
Philadelphia, designed for
Venturi's mother, 1961–4.*

Below *The Trubek and
Wislocki houses, completed
1971, on the island of
Nantucket, Massachussetts,
are modern versions of
American timber
vernacular houses.*

Opposite *The Brant and
Johnson ski lodge in Vail,
Colorado – a four-storey
tower among aspen trees,
1975–7.*

Above and right *Exterior and
interior of the Brant house
in Greenwich Connecticut,
designed in the 1970s
for a young couple with a
collection of pop art.*
Far right *The Rockefeller
house in Maine (1986) –
a classical holiday cottage.*

Above *Brunelleschi's Renaissance perspectives at the church of Santo Spirito, Florence.*

said, 'the most important result of our trip is that our group will now share a series of images and have a common basis for reference and comparison.'

The dossier for the trip to northern Italy, scheduled for May 1986, was prepared by Michael Wilson of the National Gallery, who, with the architect, explained clearly what he thought the group could gain from an immersion in Italy:

> We should think about balance between historical and modern elements in our galleries. While our ideal is to produce galleries that are architecturally analogous to the aesthetic of the paintings displayed in them and familiar, conventional, and even perhaps traditional in their forms and the associations they evoke, our spaces must also be of their own time, and must of course be workable and must maintain stringent technical and aesthetic standards that are current for lighting and environmental quality – not to mention standards that are appropriate to the crowds that attend today's museums.

Among the galleries, museums, churches and palaces visited in Italy were:

Milan: Pinacoteca di Brera, Museo Poldi-Pezzoli, Castello Sforzesco, Pinacoteca of the Biblioteca Ambrosiana.

Florence: Galleria degli Uffizi, Galleria dell'Accademia, Museo di San Marco, Palazzo Pitti, Santa Croce, Santa Maria Novella, San Lorenzo.

Siena: Pinacoteca Nazionale, Museo dell'Opera del Duomo, Palazzo Pubblico.

Venice: Galleria dell'Accademia, Palazzo Grassi, Palazzo Querini-Stampalia, Ca'd'Oro (Galleria Franchetti), Santa Maria Gloriosa dei Frari, San Zaccaria, Santi Giovanni e Paolo.

Verona: Civico Museo d'Arte di Castelvecchio.

Looking back on that journey and at the completed Sainsbury Wing, how much was learnt and what was applied?

Light in Italy was one of the things that the group particularly wanted to experience, to gauge the effect it had on the viewing of paintings. In churches and galleries there was often high side light, or the sun's rays were broken by green gauze hung over windows. In many churches darkness almost concealed the altarpieces until a 200 lire coin in the slot on the wall produced a sudden, temporary and revelatory blaze of

light. The group realised how differently we see a work of art when it is removed from its context. Devotional qualities are often lost and the display of Early Renaissance paintings in galleries both isolates and changes them. There was much discussion about the difficulties of designing a new setting for these paintings, which could never resemble their original home.

The architects were conscious of the importance of materials. In Italy there is a strong presence of stone and travertine, and on the inside of palaces and churches much use of contrasting plaster, marble and stone. There is no doubt that it was in Italy that the value and beauty of grey pietra serena was realised, especially in contrast to rough plaster walls – it was later to be used for the door-cases and skirtings of the galleries in the new wing.

There were other influences: the grand staircase of the Brera in Milan, a great Italian double stair in a neo-classical palace; the high, side-lit windows seen in many museums and palaces; marble floors, traditional floors of rectangular terracotta tiles, and floors bordered with a wide band of pietra serena; grey and white plaster walls and a much admired finish of unpainted rendered plaster known as *grassiello di calce* that seemed unique to Italy. The luminous, transparent finish to plaster walls often had a cool quality that seemed right for the sorts of paintings that the gallery planned to hang in the Sainsbury Wing. It was also little things like the clean-lined junction between stone door-cases and plaster walls that appealed, or the noble simplicity of the rooms in a museum such as San Marco in Florence. San Marco's grave elegance

was the most admired of all the settings for Early Renaissance art, but the architects warned of the dangers of re-creating 'stage-set Renaissance' in the new London galleries.

The architects made constant reference in Italian towns to the façades of churches, and sometimes to those of public buildings that consisted of grand marble or stone elements applied to the front of simple brick 'boxes'. It is interesting here to recall Vincent Scully's words in his introduction to *Complexity and Contradiction in Architecture* – he felt that Venturi's primary inspiration comes from 'the urban façades of Italy, with their endless adjustments to the counter-requirements of inside and outside and their inflection with all the business of everyday life: not primarily sculptural actors in vast landscapes, but complex spatial containers and definers of streets and squares.'

It was not expected that literal lessons should be learnt from the Italian tour but it was a vital part of the research – as had been the visits to new museums in Europe and America. It was both inspirational and practical as well as an ideal opportunity for the committee to get to understand the architect and to learn what differences might arise.

While much of the design process took place in Philadelphia, the National Gallery and its consultants developed a detailed and lengthy brief in London. During 1985 a firm of brief-coordinators and space-planners, Polkinghorne Redstall Associates, was appointed to work with the Gallery. They in turn consulted widely, involving Michael Preston of the Museum of London, Buro Happold (consulting engineers), Carr and Angier (theatre consultants), Sandy Brown Associates (acoustic consultants) and Green, Bellfield-Smith and Company (catering consultants), but their main source of research and information came from the staff of the National Gallery itself.

In this substantial document the Gallery took the opportunity to define in as much detail as possible the kind of galleries it required and how the building as a whole should function. Since it was to comprise so many disparate facilities, including galleries, a lecture theatre, a restaurant, a shop, and service areas, it was imperative to examine each in detail in order to work out how they were to operate. This information ran to 336 pages, covering such questions as security, maintenance, conservation requirements for lighting and air conditioning – as well as the technological aspects relating to them, engineering and constructional considerations, and was a full statement of the Gallery's requirements. In particular, the

Gallery made clear the kind of spaces it wanted for the paintings. Rooms with conventional features were required – a sense of permanence being thought more suitable for the Early Renaissance pictures than the free-flowing and more flexible spaces of many modern galleries. In composing the briefing document it was necessary to bring together as much factual information from National Gallery papers, visitor surveys and consultants' reports as possible. This then had to be weighed in the balance of budgetary reality and architectural possibility.

To accomplish the construction of the building a charitable company of limited liability was formed to receive the appropriate funds, develop the site and administer the project. This was to be known as The Hampton Site Company, and a subsidiary company, N. G. Services Limited, was established to control and execute the project on a day-to-day basis. The Hampton Site Company delegated its powers to a client steering committee, consisting of donors, Trustees and members of the Gallery staff, chaired by Simon Sainsbury. The Project Manager for the scheme, Eric Gabriel, was employed throughout by N. G. Services Limited. The design team was led by the architects, Venturi, Rauch and Scott Brown, Inc., who carried out all the design work in their offices in Philadelphia. The associate architect appointed in London was Sheppard Robson, who not only provided advice on UK practice and regulations but also carried out design coordination and inspection functions on the site. A Construction Manager, Sir Robert McAlpine Construction Management Ltd, was appointed to coordinate the trade contractors.

It was discussions with the steering committee (which now included the new Director of the National Gallery, Neil MacGregor, who had succeeded Sir Michael Levey in 1987), that provided the forum for the development of the design. These meetings were not always easy. In any project of this kind the development of an understanding and creative tension between architect and client is a crucial and often delicate process, but there is also a public side. Critics – royal and otherwise – have long taken a special interest in the northwest corner of Trafalgar Square.

Although detailed aspects of the architects' design were developed in response to the Gallery's brief, its fundamental features – such as the grand staircase and the layout of the galleries – remained unchanged. The way an architect solves problems is directly related to his approach to design. For this book Venturi has explained how his ideas became the reality of

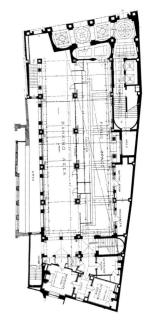

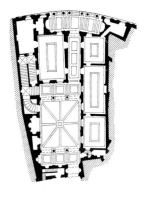

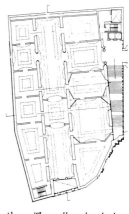

Above *The gallery level plan of The Sainsbury Wing – a complicated plan fitting alongside Wilkins's rational building.*

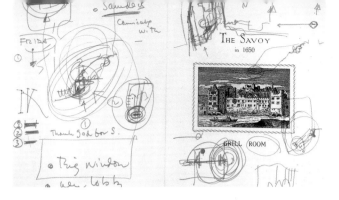

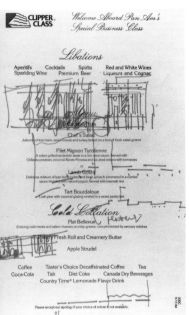

the new building. In the first place he had a special view of the site and its past. He saw it as a slice of old London rich in layers of history.

When asked how his ideas for the Sainsbury Wing were conceived, Venturi's answer is an interesting one:

To begin with the ideas are undefined, I have a penumbra of inspirational sources in my mind. I see the site as something of a metaphor. I think of medieval London lying underneath a layer of twentieth-century order. I consider the great mass of a public building in relation to the intimate personal human activities that will happen within it. Denise Scott Brown and I have always been interested in the two scales of life – the scale of the community and the scale of the individual. In the case of the National Gallery I realised that any new building had to be perfectly functional but also have a formal, public symbolic role. The idea for the façade came quickly – I saw a crescendo of columns very early on – it was refining it that took the time. When it came to the plans, I thought a lot about the way Lutyens in London had fitted his great Midland Bank building onto an awkwardly shaped City site. Look, too, at the way Wren's classical churches were made to fit old medieval sites. In Rome the great palaces are placed into a much older city plan and sometimes they are not as regular as they appear, in fact their regular rectangular grids are often quite distorted.

There were several ideas that influenced my plan for the Sainsbury Wing. I knew that in terms of the circulation of crowds everyone would have to start off at one point. From that ground-level entrance I wanted the eye to be drawn towards light. I wanted a very unambiguous stair that led up to the art – which would always be remote on a top floor but clearly accessible. I wanted the entrance hall to be a mysterious prelude – a somewhat heavy and quiet place, almost like a crypt, with something grand and light above. The materials are very important here, to suggest that sense of solidity. The firm shape of the staircase with its rusticated wall is something that does not give in – opposite it are more fascinating bulges and curves. I wanted the materials of the stair and its wall to suggest that it was an outside stair. As you go up it there are windows, and those allow you a glancing view of the art. I like the idea of catching glimpses of the art as though it is some part of a fantasy. I also think it is

important in some galleries to have occasional views of the outside world. Art is, after all, part of the world.

I know people will want to know about classicism in the new building. My use of the classical language has already received some severe criticism. But in England people have always experimented with classicism, and the use of classicism for the façade fitted into my predeliction for contextual combinations. I like the oblique view of Wilkins looking towards St Martin's, and I feel a syncopation in the build-up of columns. The power of classicism is that it can be modified and still hold its power. I learn from the way English architects have used classicism and put flesh on imported Italian bones. I like the provincial versions of the language, the naive way classicism can be adapted. I also have to say that the National Gallery would have been different if I hadn't known the work of Lutyens well.

Venturi's ideas slowly became reality, although certain changes inevitably happened. Initially, the windows were to be bronze, white marble floors were suggested for the galleries, and the whole of the exterior of the building was to be clad in Portland stone. A plan for much more extensive excavation to create a variety of rooms under Jubilee Walk had to be rejected on the grounds of expense. The proposed studio for an artist in residence was abandoned; the location of the temporary exhibition area had to be moved below ground; and the number of loading bays was much debated. Venturi described this part of the process of architecture as 'editing the wish list', a sometimes very intense process that leads both architect and client into the light of reality.

Just before the exhibition of the final scheme Venturi had given a public lecture – The Cubitt Lecture – at the Royal Society of Arts, London, in which he explained to a professional audience his philosophy and approach to the National Gallery extension. The spatial complexity of gallery design had, he felt, a lot to do with the large didactic element that is present in any modern art museum programme. The changing nature of collections and the need to provide mechanically efficient and relatively neutral spaces for changing exhibitions made the brief for any modern gallery very different from one given in the nineteenth century. Although Venturi said that he considered it the architect's and the engineer's job to solve the Chinese puzzle aspect of museum planning on a narrow and irregular urban site, he admitted

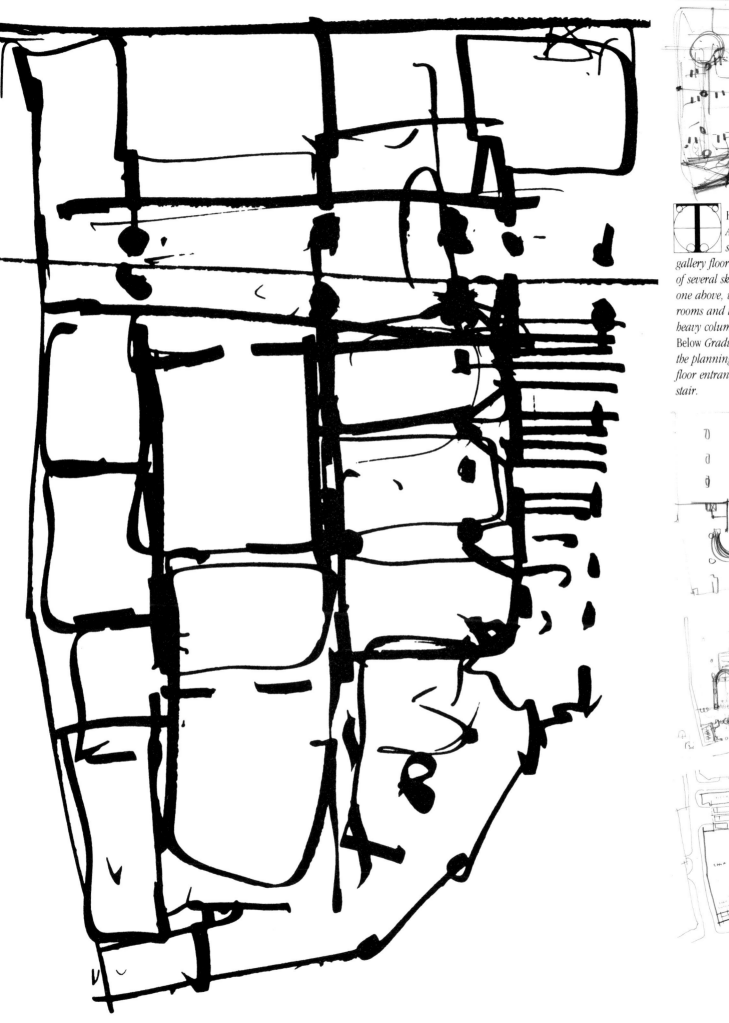

THE PLAN
*A clear early
sketch of the
gallery floor* (left) *grew out
of several sketches like the
one above, which shows the
rooms and the structure of
heavy columns.*
Below Gradual resolution of
*the planning of the ground
floor entrance hall and
stair.*

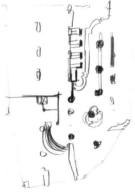

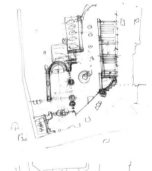

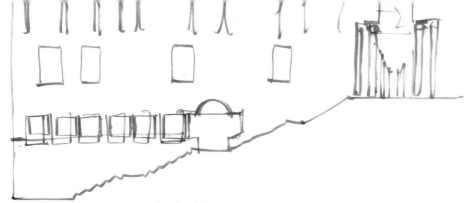

that he felt the complexity of the Sainsbury Wing needed the skills and refinement of a Swiss watchmaker.

Art, Venturi felt, sometimes seems remote in modern museums because of all the other activities that are going on around it. In some of the large American museums, and some museums in France, the visitor may occasionally wonder whether he is not visiting a major department store or has just arrived at the airport. Venturi has dealt with this problem in London by means of hierarchy and scale. In the entrance lobby the visitor is first struck by the large architectural forms, whose generous scale suggests that he is entering an institutional building. The grand single-flight staircase makes it very clear that the way to the art galleries is up. There is no maze of medium-sized elements; the hierarchy is clear inside, and the scale and materials outside suggest a civic and public building.

When it came to the design of the galleries themselves, Venturi's views were unequivocal: 'The galleries should be rooms for looking at paintings in, not contraptions for containing them. The architecture should not overshadow the art.' In the Sainsbury Wing they also had to be capable of allowing very large numbers of people to look at some works of art that are relatively small; the architectural detail in the galleries needed therefore to be refined and simple.

The outside of a public gallery, however, does require some presence. This can be a problem when the gallery is in a thriving commercial city where the surrounding office blocks are so much larger – somehow the gallery has to be a small building designed with a sense of grand scale. It has the added task of appearing welcoming. A skilful breaking down of elements can achieve this, as can be seen on the Whitcomb Street elevation, which has shop windows and elegant colonettes against the stone base to decrease the bulky scale of the building and to add interest at eye level for the passer-by. Venturi had entitled his lecture at the Royal Society of Arts 'From Invention to Convention in Architecture'; the opportunity for the general public to see the architectural expression of these ideas was to come at the exhibition of the final scheme plans.

Because of the year-long development period for the brief and the design, it was not until April 1987 that a public exhibition of the completed scheme was held at the National Gallery. The design, of course, had already been through the complex internal approval procedures of the Gallery. To satisfy as diverse a group as the National Gallery staff and Trustees was not without its difficulties; architecture in the late twentieth century is fraught with potential for discord, for pluralism allows a diversity of views. As far as Venturi's creative struggle was concerned, it produced what he referred to at the opening of the exhibition as 'a rich and rewarding dialogue'. A year before he had said that he was the happiest architect in the world, and the most privileged. At the press preview of the design he announced that he still felt the same way.

T HE GALLERIES
Three sketch ideas
(left and right)
and perspective drawing
(below) *of the two main
gallery vistas. Venturi
originally wanted his main
vista to end in a large
window looking out to the
top of the portico of Canada
House* (below right); *it now
has a painting as its focus.*
Bottom right *Sketch of the
profile of the skirting
mouldings used throughout
the galleries.*

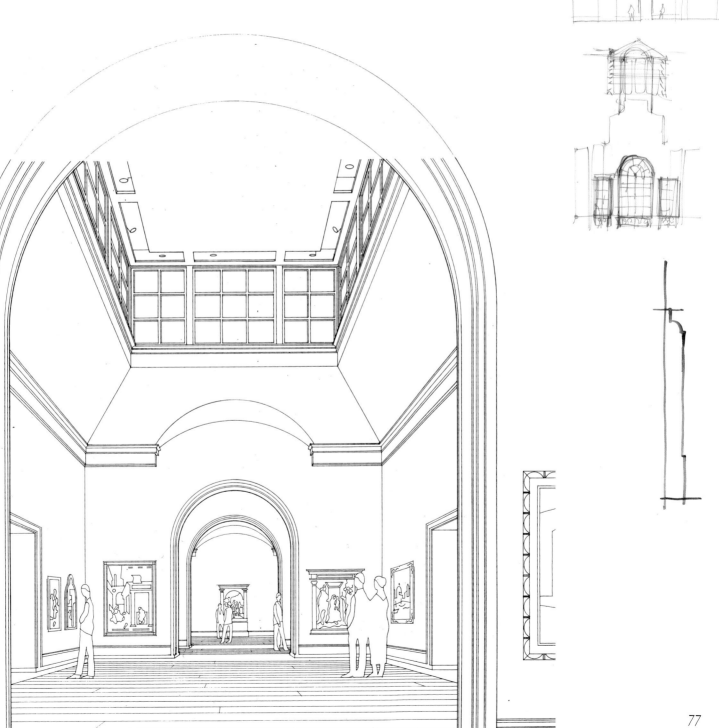

77

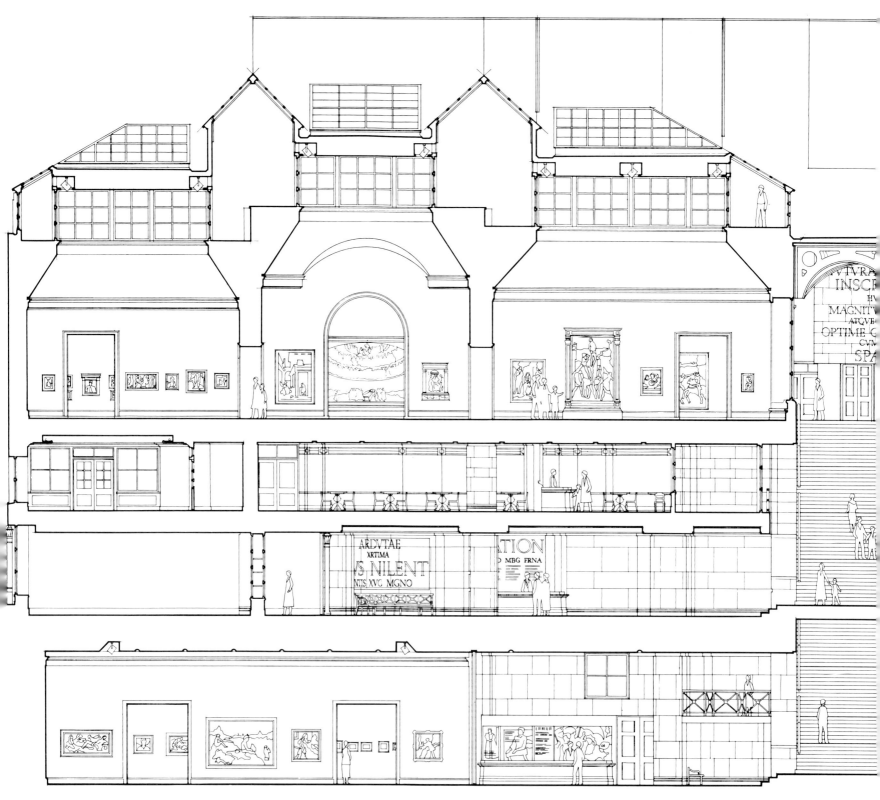

Within the drawing, the following inscriptions are visible:

VIVRA
INSC
HV
MAGNIT
ATQVE
OPTIME
CVM
SPA

ARDVTAE
XRTIMA
VS NILENT
NTIS XVG MGNO

ATION
O MBG FRNA

Transverse section of the wing showing every level and the link to the main building.

In the exhibition – itself designed by the architects – the salient points of the developed scheme were clearly shown. Models and drawings were on view for more than a month. Public comment was invited as well as the views of the appropriate design and conservationist quangos.

Venturi, discussing his firm's approach, said that they had decided to respect the style of Wilkins's building – the 'much loved friend'. They had done this by speaking the classical language with columns and pilasters as part of their vocabulary. 'Far from being subservient, however, we hope you will agree we have created a building of its own time.'

He also reiterated the age-old problem of the Hampton site – one that had dogged all previous competitions – which is that of a narrow site demanding a predominantly vertical arrangement adjoining a set of rooms (the main galleries) that run on a long horizontal enfilade. To solve this problem, and to achieve a set of fine top-lit galleries on the same level and linked to the Wilkins building, necessitated very tight planning of all the other spaces. Venturi explained the strong vertical arrangement: the loading bay for the huge service vehicles sits on top of the lecture theatre, while above it is the computer room, which is in turn below one of the main

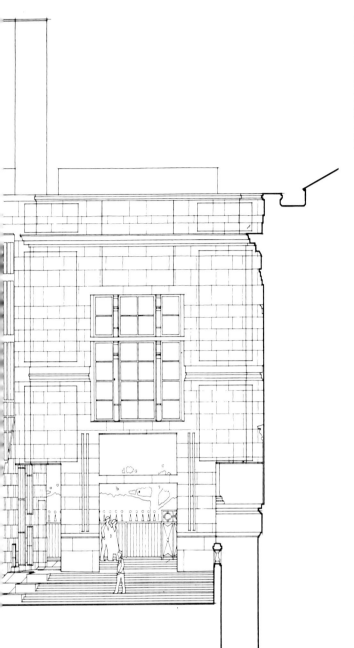

chapels or palace rooms,' he said, 'but should recall instead the substantial architectural character and the air of permanence of these places. In these galleries the most exquisite small paintings must look at home yet vast crowds must be able to circulate freely.'

The National Gallery monitored the exhibition, which had 74,607 visitors. Questionnaires were handed out, and many of them were returned with comments, as requested, to the Westminster planning office. There were more positive than negative comments, the majority approving of the building's sympathetic relationship with Trafalgar Square.

One of the official quangos, the Royal Fine Art Commission, visited the exhibition and commented, 'we are very impressed by the fine concept of Venturi's design, which pays due deference to Wilkins's National Gallery, links up with it and at the same time provides a good example of contemporary architecture.'

The press had always taken an interest in the National Gallery's architecture since the Prince of Wales had so forcefully expressed his views on the 'carbuncle' scheme. They were waiting eagerly for the Venturi design to be unveiled, and their reactions were as full of variety as the design itself. *The Sunday Times* was very enthusiastic: Simon Jenkins wrote with memorable excitement, showing perhaps how Venturi had skilfully judged his lay audience, rather than the tendentious architectural critics:

> It is a triumph, a dazzling display. . . . Inside the new gallery is a celebration not just of the Renaissance but of the rebirth of the city, portrayed in the backgrounds of so many of its pictures. In the main galleries, there are more columns, arches, perspectives and historical allusions to frame the work of Piero and Uccello and Bellini and Cranach and van Eyck. Below, more recent examples of revivalism are celebrated: coloured Victorian railway columns in the foyer and a huge Crystal Palace vault over the grand staircase. This is not the frigid classical revival of Paris's Grand Palais or the art mausolea of Washington. It is an intimate, humorous variation on a renaissance theme of the kind that has been the inspiration of English architects from Inigo Jones to Edwin Lutyens. . . . Designed by an American in the European classical tradition it contains no trace of chauvinism. It revives architectural humanism and carries it forward with bravura. May it be widely imitated.

galleries. The new Sainsbury Wing increases the existing gallery space by a quarter, but the demand for many ancillary spaces and activities points up the difference between modern museums and those of the nineteenth century. Venturi pointed out that the ratio of art versus support space was 9:1 in the nineteenth century, but 1:2 in the late twentieth century.

Venturi's architecture does not dominate the art collection. His high light lanterns aim to give not a dead museum light but a lively, safe level of daylight, and the rooms are subtly designed to provide 'an associative context' for the pictures. 'We feel that the gallery setting should not replicate

Right *The final form of the main façade grew from a series of cardboard models – pilasters and columns came and went until harmony was reached.* Opposite *Architects' sketch of a capital for the new wing.* Opposite below *Capitals copied from the Wilkins building.*

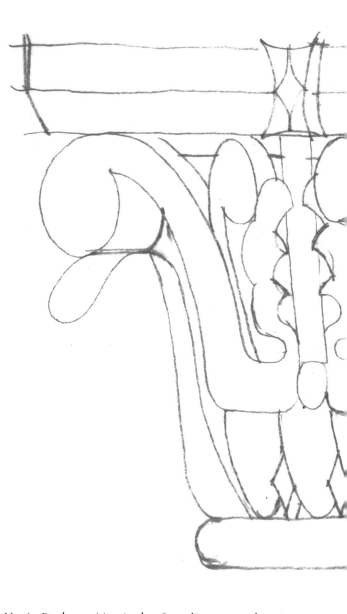

Martin Pawley, writing in the *Guardian*, was welcoming too:

> Given the constraints of the brief, Venturi, Rauch and Scott Brown have succeeded in creating dignity and authority where some critics expected weakness and compromise. If there is any justice left in Trafalgar Square this one should be built.

The President of the Royal Institute of British Architects applauded the design – an unusual step for an architect:

> Here we have a clever two in one solution – a fitting thoughtful design following the building line in Portland stone with careful classical detailing. Yet it is in no way a pastiche, essentially it is a completely modern and original approach.

There was also considerable press coverage in the United States, where Venturi had been known for far longer than he, or his firm, had been in England. Paul Goldberger, writing in the *New York Times*, was enthusiastic:

> The architectural dilemma was to create a building that would be many things at once. It would have to have sufficient presence to be an element on its own in

Trafalgar Square yet it would also have to contribute something toward pulling the mix of buildings on the square together. And it would have to relate comfortably to the original National Gallery building without either dominating it or being dominated by it.

The Venturi design appears to succeed at striking this difficult and tremendously subtle balance. It is different on all of its sides, to inflect toward the different buildings that surround it, yet it is also a coherent whole. The building is a case of classicism transformed, a design that is clearly of the late twentieth century and not of any other period. But this is the late twentieth century trying not so much to abandon classicism as to make its own comment on it.

In the *Wall Street Journal* later that year, under the heading 'New ideas from an ex-enfant terrible', Ellen Posner described the National Gallery plans as 'an elegantly worked out solution to contemporary museum problems, the Venturi design proposes a broad interior stair (a "grand ascent") running along one glass-walled side of the building. It would shoot visitors past food, shopping and entertainment, directly to the room-like galleries above.'

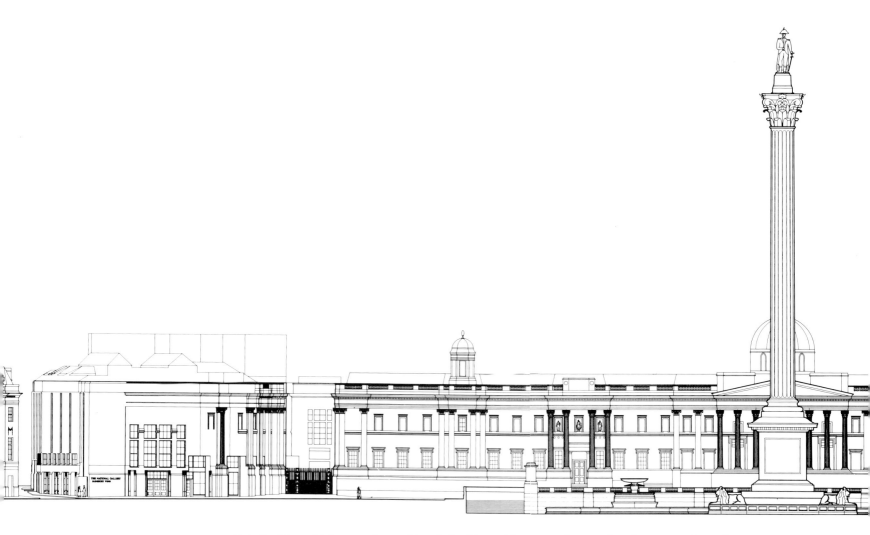

Not all of the criticism was favourable – indeed it would have been surprising if it had been. What many critics fail to realise is that Venturi welcomes reasonable criticism and enjoys it. He happily accepted criticism of his own work from his students at Princeton: 'Sure, why not? It's only architecture, not religion.' And he has always questioned the heroic idea of the modern architect as the man with the only right answer. Often the hard-line modernists have failed to understand the gentle but pertinent questioning that is apparent in every aspect of Venturi's architecture. He is prepared for disagreement, although it does not follow that he is prepared to change his approach.

The *Architectural Review* was one of the fiercest critics of the design. In the June 1987 issue, the critic E. M. Farrelly referred to Venturi's determination to love the Wilkins building and base his façade design upon it:

It is one of the greatnesses of love to find beauty where others see only dross, and Venturi went on to praise for its elegance and subtle rhythms a façade which other critics – Summerson, for one – have considered over theatrical, ambiguous and trivialised by fussiness, and to draw historical precedent from almost any source – Soane, Gibbs, Lutyens, Paxton, and Italian Renaissance palazzi in general – that might provide for the new building the kind of European classical pedigree Venturi so clearly feels it needs.

In this – rather desperate, eclectic historicism – as in so much else about the building, the book provides the clue. *Complexity and Contradiction in Architecture* was written more than 20 years ago, but it remains one of the most important, influential and powerfully argued books ever written on architecture. To its determined and, then, heretical advocacy of pluralism, eclecticism and decoration in architecture, and its attack on what was seen to be the poverty of modernism, can be traced much of what has happened in architecture since. And while much of that may be regrettable, it is nonetheless one of those occasional theoretical treatises which, at a certain point in history, need – demand – to be written. If Venturi hadn't written it, somebody else would have had to.

Such 20-year loyalty to a particular set of ideas may, perhaps, be a sign of strength. What is disturbing, though, is their evident lack of development over time: nowhere, in neither the argument nor the building, does one sense that gradual deepening or fleshing-out that can turn a clever academic idea into a full-blooded architectural one. Even good ideas do not necessarily make good buildings; on the contrary, too many ideas improperly digested can merely increase the confusion. And that, one feels, is what has happened here, replacing that High-Renaissance generosity that Venturi clearly seeks with the papery thinness and too clever fragility of Mannerism.

Discussing the Venturi façade on Trafalgar Square in particular, Farrelly writes:

> Mannerism . . . is not itself a crime, but it is a demanding style, and to work at all it must be done well. The National Gallery extension, as proposed, is full of Mannerist tricks and jokes of every kind, but few jokes – only the really first rate, splendidly told – can stand the telling more than once. And these are not, on the whole, first rate. What happens when, paper thin from the start, they begin to wear out? How long before we simply tire of the National's clever kid brother, who insists on being around, but will not be quiet?

There were other critical articles, many of them by critics who simply did not want to understand the difficulties of the site and the brief. It was Deyan Sudjic who wrote in the now defunct *London Daily News*, in April 1987, how accurately he felt Venturi's design reflected the current architectural mood:

> Venturi's design shows enough promise to be a much better building than we could have dared to hope for at one time. On the other hand, to a future generation it will speak embarrassingly frankly about the mannered and schizophrenic approach to architecture in the 1980s.

As Venturi has often said during the design and building of the gallery, 'architecture gets you into a lot of trouble.'

Venturi had given his lecture at the Royal Society of Arts the title 'From Invention to Convention in Architecture', and it had been a cogent analysis of current architectural thinking. He had, he admitted, raised a lot more questions than he had given answers, but that was the nature of the subject. The urban art museum did indeed raise many questions – 'it had to be popular and esoteric, it had to be monumental yet inviting, an accommodating setting for the art but a work of art in itself' – all of which the Sainsbury Wing tackled and brought to the fore. How successfully some or all of these questions have been answered is for the visitor to judge.

THE CONTEXT
Above *The architects' submission drawing showing the new wing in relation to Trafalgar Square.* Below *Perspective drawing showing the new wing as a natural extension of the existing Gallery.*

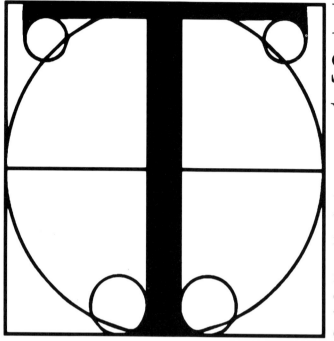

CHAPTER 5

THE NEW SAINSBURY WING

The Sainsbury Wing is a building full of ideas, but just how have these ideas been turned into architecture? It is worth beginning from the outside, gradually examining the building as it stands with some of the architects' concepts in mind.

The outside of the new wing relates to its urban context, in some ways reflecting it, and in other ways acting as a counterpoint. Venturi has said that the new building is something of a 'fragment of the old'. This is true because the new entrance façade, seen from the square, echoes the height, material and some of the major classical elements of Wilkins's building. The closely packed pilasters at the eastern end of the new façade look as though they have been drawn back and folded away, like a screen. They have been pushed up close to the main building – a friendly gathering of older elements keeping their distance from the plainer and purer Pall Mall palazzo front that extends away to the west.

Behind this cut and carved stone screen is another wall, a layer of glass, through which the visitor walks to reach the public entrance hall. As you pass under the cut-out arch in the stone wall, a glance to your right will find the best sequence of columns, pilasters and porticoes in London. This view, looking past the bronze stomach of King James II towards Gibbs's spire of St Martin-in-the-Fields, is thrilling. It is worth remembering how unexpected it must have seemed when Gibbs placed a medieval spire on top of a classical portico – something of a contradiction indeed. Such a vista is also a perfect example of what Venturi so rightly calls 'London's friendly grandeur'.

Once you have passed from York stone pavement through the revolving door into the entrance hall, pause for a moment and contemplate the scale and solidity of this hall. Five fat columns firmly divide the space on the right. They seem like squat supporters of some great cathedral – are they bearing the weight of the whole of the Renaissance? A slow progression through this impressive stone hall reveals its more sinuous side. The west wall past the shop is made up of a series of sensuous curves – there is something comfortable and

Opposite King James II looks *well pleased with his newest neighbour.*

welcoming about the curved bench in the curved niche. It is in great contrast to the rusticated stone wall opposite, which gives the impression of a strong man contemplating his softer, more feminine neighbour.

The great tour de force of the new wing awaits on the east side of the foyer. From the low stone hall, a few paces brings you to the foot of the grand staircase. Quite suddenly you receive a splendid sense of space, height and dignity. There, seen through the glass curtain wall, is the solid wall of Wilkins's gallery and the whirl of life in Trafalgar Square. But as you look ahead up the seemingly steep flight of granite stairs there is a solemn sense of grandeur. Other great staircases come to mind – the climb at the Brera in Milan, the long march in Munich's Alte Pinakothek, or the sublime Scala Regia in the Vatican – but all of them aspire, and give the visitor a moment to prepare for contemplation. As you climb slowly out of the everyday world, it is appropriate that the walls are sheer sheets of cut stone – blank except for the incised names of great artists – the mind is cleared for the feast ahead. The stairway does offer its own surprises, however. Look up from the bottom and sense the shortened perspective; look down and the staircase suddenly seems to be surprisingly long.

There is a strong architectural logic in the arrangement of the grand staircase and its adjoining public circulation spaces. On the first floor the visitor can leave the stair on the way to the galleries and enjoy a visit to the Micro Gallery with its computer information facilities. It is on this level that the restaurant and coffee bar are located. The restaurant has intriguing views of Trafalgar Square as well as paintings by Paula Rego, based on themes from Early Renaissance paintings in the National Gallery Collection. On this floor there are conference and meeting rooms and a small dining room.

There are two more enjoyable architectural surprises to be found at the top of the great staircase. Once you have arrived on the gallery floor you are on the same level as the main rooms of the old National Gallery, although it seems that you have climbed much further. To the east is the circular link that bridges Jubilee Walk, but look beyond it and there is a complete enfilade through some of the main rooms of the National Gallery. The circular room that spans Jubilee Walk has grand windows that give views north to the new garden and south to Trafalgar Square.

The view to the west from the top of the grand staircase is of an unusual diminishing perspective framed by giant columns of grey pietra serena. This vista is appropriately terminated by the Cima altarpiece – which appears to continue in its painting of a coffered ceiling this same diminishing perspective. One is reminded here of views inside Florentine churches. Venturi does not presume to imitate, though he does remind the visitor that architecture has a history, that there are connexions.

The gallery floor itself is a singular achievement because it appears to create more space than would have seemed possible on this narrow site. This is no free-flowing space but a series of rooms with grandly scaled doors, arched openings and tall windows. As originally suggested by the Gallery in their brief for the 1982 competition, their arrangement is rather processional, with the main central aisle enhancing the feeling of a great basilican space. The grey walls, darker grey pietra serena door-cases, skirtings and borders to the oak floors all contribute to the overall atmosphere of dignity and serenity. Clearly the spirit of Sir John Soane walks in these galleries, for they are very similar to his rooms at Dulwich Picture Gallery. There are the same lunettes in the ceilings, the same wide curved arches between the main rooms. The walls are plain, the ceilings complex – their complexity determined by the lighting. Above the galleries is a floor of lighting controls, skylights and louvres that let in as much light as is safe for the delicate paintings. But all that is visible from the galleries themselves is a series of elegant lanterns with etched-glass windows.

On the eastern side are four giant windows that look into the great stairway and out onto the world of London. They are architecturally powerful in scale, and the eye is drawn from framed visions as realised by the Renaissance artists to the architecturally framed confusions of life in the present-day temporal world. These views out of the 'layered' building are an important aspect of the architects' scheme. It is an architectural theme that Venturi has developed since he designed his mother's house in Philadelphia (1961–4). A recurrent feature, these framed views are constantly intriguing and rewarding. On the first floor, on the way to the restaurant, the variety of glimpses of Nelson's Column, pigeons, fountains and traffic is enthralling.

Quite a different experience is to be had on the way down the great staircase to the lower depths of the new wing, where the lecture theatre and temporary exhibition galleries are to be found. The stair changes its entire character on its descent from the entrance hall to the lower floors. Shades of the granite vaults of Lutyens's Castle Drogo are combined with

The architect invented a particularly solid version of the Tuscan Order to emphasise the diminishing perspective of the main east-west axis of the galleries.

Light is the key to the design of the galleries – not a dead artificial light but a controlled system of daylight from handsome lofty lanterns that allow glimpses of the sky.

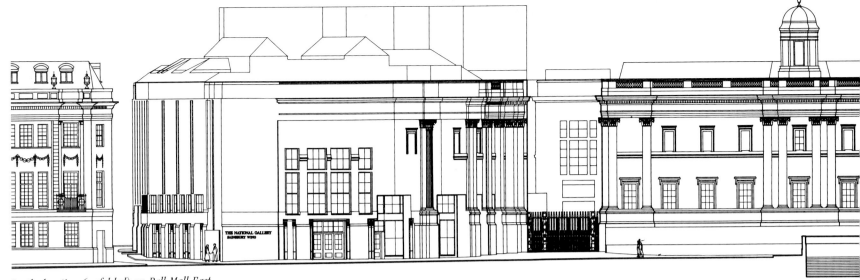

South elevation (unfolded) on Pall Mall East.

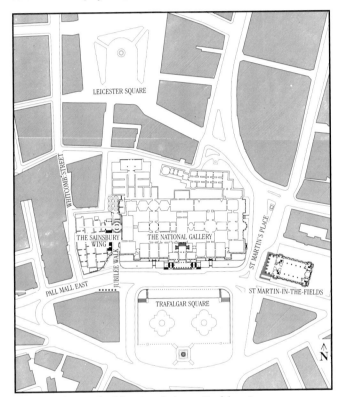

Site plan, the new building in relation to Trafalgar Square.

FLOOR PLANS

GALLERY WALL AREAS
measurements given in square metres

Level 5 main galleries/east	742
Level 5 main galleries/central	662
Level 5 main galleries/west	649
Level 1 temporary exhibition galleries	735
TOTAL	2,788

PICTURE HANGING SPACE
measurements given in linear metres

Main galleries	450
Temporary exhibition galleries	200
TOTAL	650

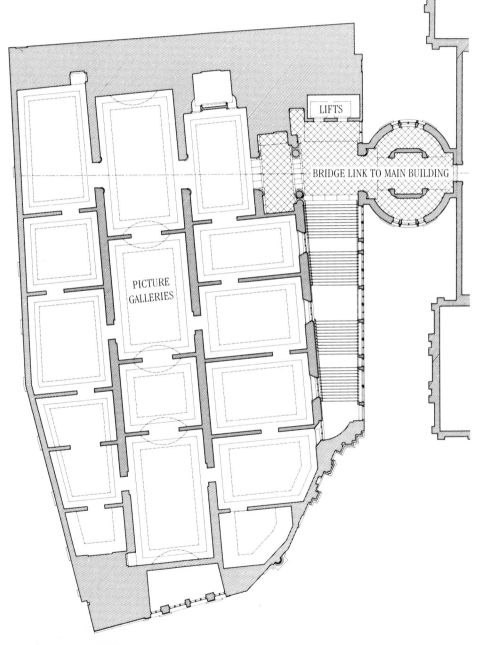

Level 5 MAIN FLOOR
Sixteen galleries of various sizes linked to Wilkins's building
by a circular room spanning Jubilee Walk.
(Pages 89–95 Architects' plans updated as built.)

Opposite *References to history have their place in Venturi's design and the inspiration of Sir John Soane's Dulwich Picture Gallery (1811–14) is clear in this view of the arches and lunettes of the main galleries. Carefully detailed elements – door cases, cornices and skirtings – are the only restrained ornament in rooms intended for the quiet contemplation of pictures.*
Above right *Michael Harvey, carver and lettering artist, hand carved a frieze of artists' names on the grand staircase.*
Centre right *The swollen Tuscan capital of one of the pietra serena columns on the gallery floor.*
Below right *'God is the details' – fine quality of workmanship on the cut granite of the grand staircase.*

East elevation on Jubilee Walk.

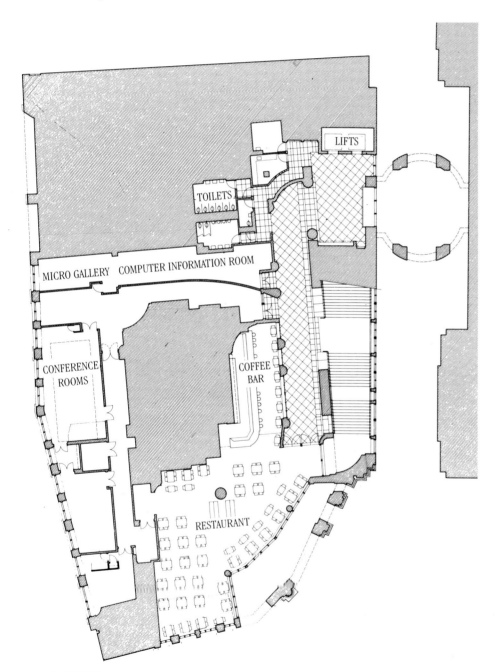

MICRO GALLERY COMPUTER INFORMATION ROOM

LIFTS

TOILETS

CONFERENCE ROOMS

COFFEE BAR

RESTAURANT

Level 4 FIRST FLOOR

Restaurant, coffee bar, Micro Gallery computer information room, conference rooms, lifts, public toilets, first-aid and parent-infant rooms.

GROSS FLOOR AREAS

measurements given in square metres

Level 1/Basement	2,344
Level 2/Lower ground floor	809
Level 3/Ground floor	2,237
Level 4/First floor	1,991
Level 5/Main floor	2,304
Bridge	108
Voids	569
Entrance arcade	209
Roof plant	985
TOTAL	11,556

SCHEDULE OF AREAS OF PUBLIC SPACES

measurements given in square metres

Main galleries	1,408
Temporary exhibition galleries	475
Audio-visual cinema (*seats 50*)	38
Lecture theatre (*seats 340*)	360
Entrance foyer	589
Shop	380
Grand staircase	190
Lower main staircase	111
Conference rooms	164
Restaurant	245
Coffee bar	84
Computer information room	101
Bridge link	108
TOTAL	4,253

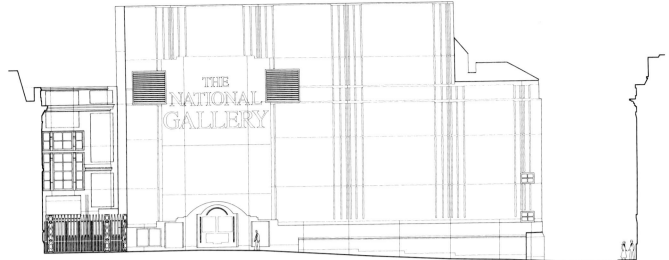

North elevation on St Martin's Street.

a reminder of the giant plaster cornice of his Viceroy's House in New Delhi. The intricacy of the vertical planning and the skill of the excavation and construction become apparent as you realise that the lecture theatre, cinema and temporary exhibition galleries all occupy space below ground level. During the excavation there was a real sense of almost Piranesian grandeur in the character of the huge caves that had to be dug in the London clay.

The 340-seat lecture theatre on the lower ground floor and the small audio-visual cinema in the basement provide the National Gallery with excellent facilities for its public education programme. And the basement suite of six temporary exhibition rooms, for the first time, allows the Gallery to house visiting exhibitions in air-conditioned space. They are approached via a beautifully simple circular lobby, a fine high space with a counter for the purchase of catalogues. The temporary galleries themselves fulfil the Gallery's criteria for a set of straightforward rooms: they are varied in scale so that they can be used in different combinations; there is no natural light; and the wall surfaces can be altered and the rooms 'furnished' to suit the content and character of each exhibition. At the back of the exhibition galleries there is a linking passage to the picture store, picture lifts and loading bays.

The intricacy made necessary by having to squeeze as much as possible onto the last remaining site on Trafalgar Square is almost visible on the mezzanine levels – the lower ground and first floors. Inevitably their ceiling heights have had to be limited. It is salutary to think that the kitchens and restaurant lie immediately beneath rooms containing some of the world's finest paintings. The visitor should not be aware of the complex services necessary to maintain precise conditions of humidity, temperature and light. But they played a vital role in the design of the building, for it is all these elements that ensure a completely modern environment for the paintings.

The construction of the new wing was inevitably a complicated process because of the nature of the institution, the active involvement of the donors, and the fact that the architects were designing and producing the working drawings some 3,000 miles away in Philadelphia. Once a building is

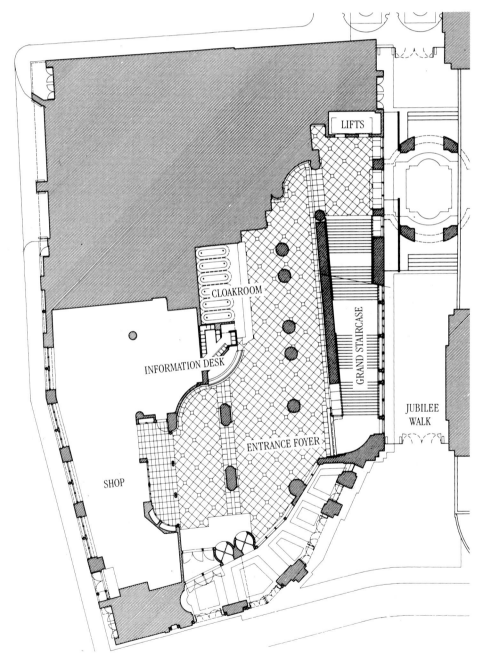

Level 3 GROUND FLOOR
The grand staircase, gallery shop (with a separate entrance in Whitcomb Street), information desk, cloakrooms, lifts, service areas and main loading area.

Above *The lecture theatre on the lower ground floor seats 340 people and is fully equipped for staged events as well as slide lectures.*

Right *A small cinema has been tucked into a space beneath the lecture theatre, off the exhibitions foyer.*

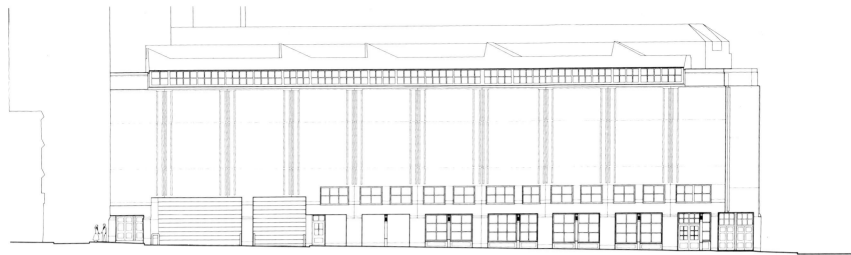

West elevation on Whitcomb Street.

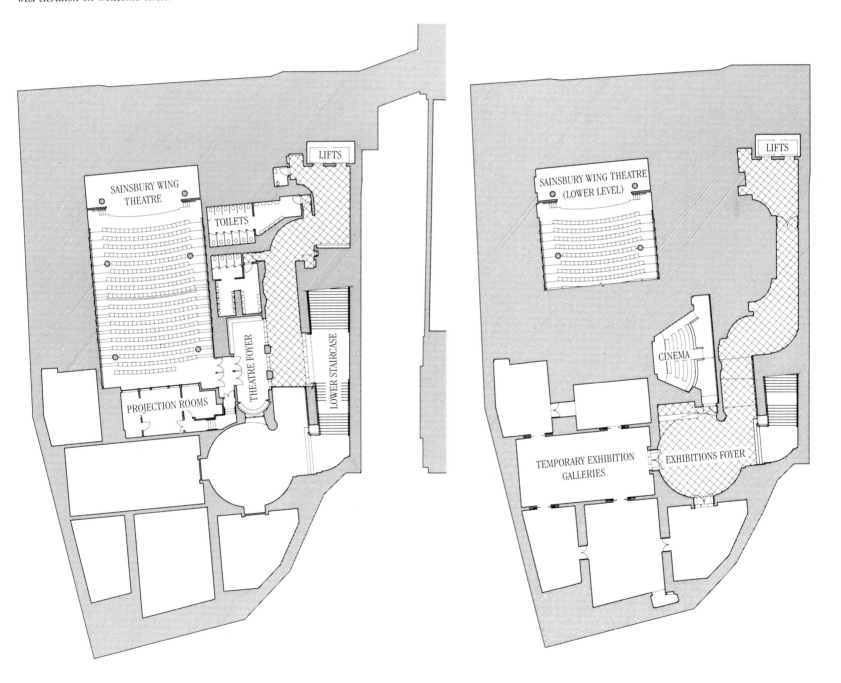

LIFTS

SAINSBURY WING
THEATRE

TOILETS

THEATRE FOYER

PROJECTION ROOMS

LOWER STAIRCASE

LIFTS

SAINSBURY WING THEATRE
(LOWER LEVEL)

CINEMA

TEMPORARY EXHIBITION
GALLERIES

EXHIBITIONS FOYER

Level 2 LOWER GROUND FLOOR
Lecture theatre (equipped with full sound and projection
facilities); public toilets.

Level 1 BASEMENT
Temporary exhibition galleries (six rooms); small cinema;
service areas and staff rooms.

Opposite above *Sinuous curved stone walls reinforce the almost Piranesian quality of the undercroft-like entrance hall.*
Opposite below *The new bookshop has the air of a handsome library with space to browse as well as buy.*
Right *There is a sense of generous space in the lower floors, which were excavated into the depths of the London clay: the circular foyer outside the temporary exhibition galleries, and (below) the foot of the lower staircase. The balcony of the lecture theatre foyer on the lower ground floor overlooks the exhibitions foyer at basement level.*

A view of the National
Gallery that puts the
Sainsbury Wing into
perspective. Such a relatively
small new building has
been the focus of so much
attention because of the
prominence of the site.

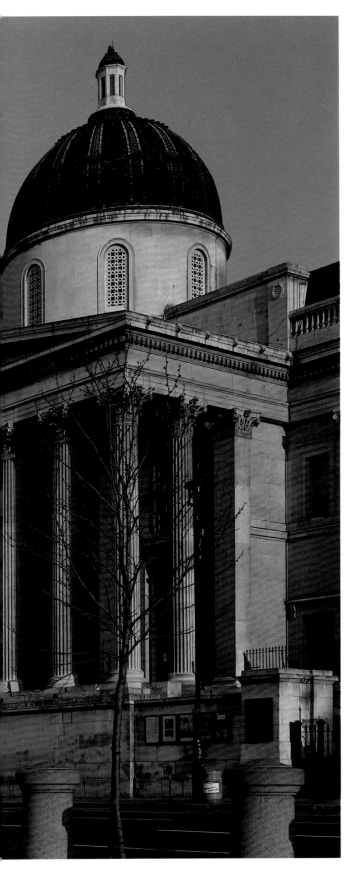

completed much of the process is inevitably forgotten – as a painful labour is forgotten the moment a child is born. The distance between the architects and the job was, to some extent, alleviated by the existence of the fax machine. Perhaps one day the faxes exchanged between London and Philadelphia will be published. They would make a remarkable file.

The late twentieth century brings together a cosmopolitan workforce to achieve the completion of any contemporary building – public or private. The Sainsbury Wing was no exception: Portuguese stonemasons worked on stone cut in France; some of the joiners and carpenters were Sikhs; both the architect and the lighting expert came from the United States; the pietra serena stone used for the columns, doorways and gallery surrounds came from Italy, and the granite for the stairs from Cold Spring, USA. The full technical details of the construction are detailed on pages 132–6.

The elements were kind to the building programme – the long, hot summer of 1990 tanned the workforce and made long hours of work possible. The full-scale mock-up of a gallery that had been built at Shepperton to test the lighting was soon replaced by the building itself. Committee after committee met and met again. The core client steering group lived and breathed the Sainsbury Wing to an extent that is impossible to explain to anyone who was not involved.

Apart from the wonders of the new building itself and the great success of the architects' design, the achievement of the Sainsbury Wing lies also in the process that built it. The political climate of the 1980s brought vigorous private interest to national museums and galleries; new donors were able to prove that perpetual public parsimony could be overcome by private effort. A donation such as the Sainsbury Wing is a rare thing, but it is worth recording that it also brought the National Gallery a group of committed friends with energy and determination and a record of practical achievement. The new wing is a monument to the revival of private patronage as well as a superb addition to the Gallery, and an important example of the architecture of its time. The history of the Hampton site, told here, shows how often Government control combined with a terrible rationing of funds has made life ceaselessly difficult for the National Gallery. The Sainsbury Wing broke the stalemate and could easily become an example to others. It is a wonderful gift to the nation.

*Reflections on classicism –
the stone façade of the new
wing is a modulated essay
that develops the theme of
the pilaster and column
from the original Wilkins
building. It is a piece of
London stage scenery.*

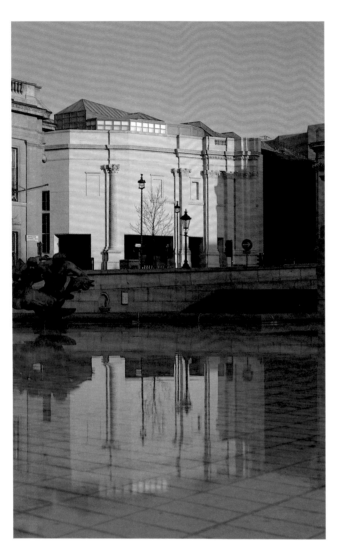

The new building has been described as resembling a slice of beautifully iced cake that has been cut from the old building and pushed a little to one side, revealing through its dark glass wall the riches inside. This view looks towards the circular linking building that bridges Jubilee Walk.

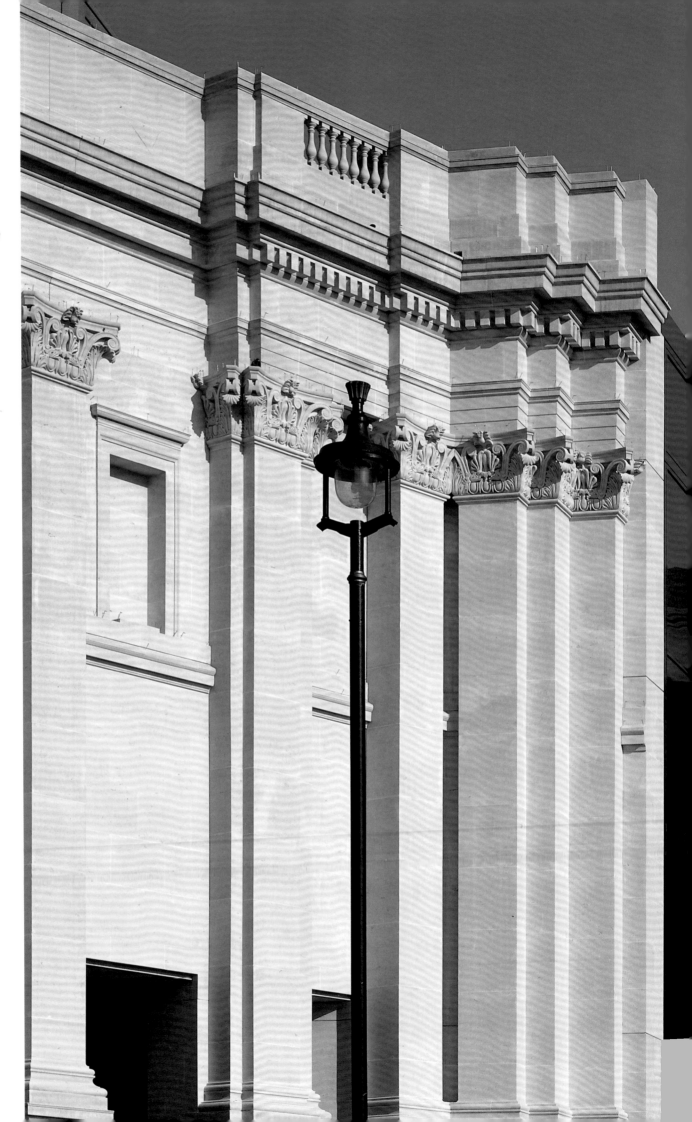

Left *The new wing closely
observed from Pall Mall
East, and* (below) *seen from
the portico of the main
building, clearly revealing
the giant openings that
mark the entrance.*

Overleaf *Two views looking up and down the grand stair. This imposing element of the design is rich in references – from the Scala Regia to Victorian engineering.*

Opposite *Jubilee Walk, now much enhanced, passes under Venturi's circular bridge link.*
Below *A giant Pall Mall clubland window is appropriate for the south façade.*

Opposite *Looking west from the first room on the gallery floor along the diminishing perspective towards the Cima altarpiece,* The Incredulity of Saint Thomas.

Above *Uccello's famous* Battle of San Romano *is seen through the doorway of Room 54; to the left of the doorway is Masaccio's* Virgin and Child, *and to the right is Gentile da Fabriano's* Madonna and Child with Angels.

Two great Crivelli paintings hang in Room 57: to the left the altarpiece known as The Madonna della Rondine *shows the Virgin and Child with Saint Jerome and Saint Sebastian; to the right is* The Vision of the Blessed Gabriele.

An oblique and a direct view of Raphael's Crucified Christ, *which hangs at the north end of the central range of galleries.*

Right *Lorenzo Monaco's
altarpiece of* The Coronation
of the Virgin with adoring
Saints *occupies one wall of
Room 54 with two
fragments of its predella. On
the right wall are Sassetta's*
Scenes from the Life of Saint
Francis, *completed in 1444.
On the left wall Gentile da
Fabriano's* Madonna and
Child with Angels *hangs
alongside four predella
panels from an altarpiece
by Giovanni di Paolo.*
Above *The new galleries
allow an intriguing series of
views and juxtapositions of
paintings. Here, beyond* The
Annunciation *by Fra Filippo
Lippi in Room 55, to the left,
can be glimpsed Bellini's*
Agony in the Garden *in
Room 57.*

Overleaf left *The central vista of the new galleries looking south towards* The Demidoff Altarpiece.
Overleaf right *Piero della Francesca's* The Baptism of Christ *hangs in a special room dedicated to this artist's work.*

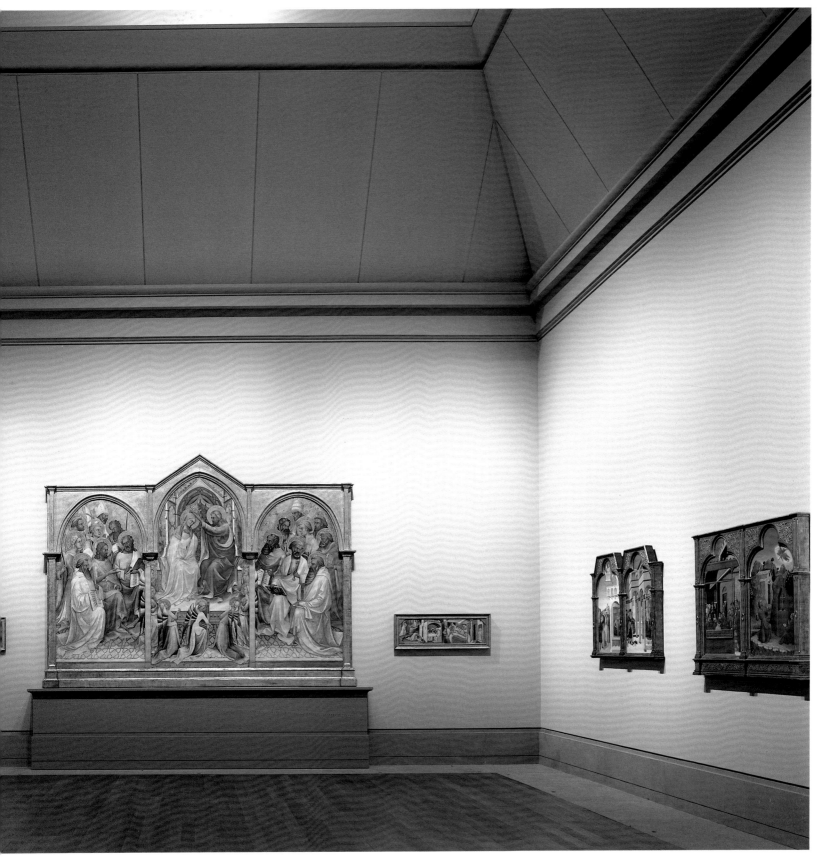

665. THE BAPTISM
BY PIERO DELLA FRANCESCA c 1410-1492, UMBRIAN SCHOOL.

One of the grandest vistas in any art gallery has been revealed by the alignment of the new wing with the galleries of the main building – seen here looking east from the circular bridge link.

Boldly detailed giant cornices add a sense of scale and drama to the descent to the lower floors.

Below *The restaurant has fine views over Trafalgar Square and close-up glimpses of Canada House.* Right *The new wing is full of opportunities for surprise views of London – Nelson's column seen from the staircase.*

THE EARLY RENAISSANCE COLLECTION

The National Gallery's magnificent Early Renaissance collection, which spans the period 1260 to 1510 and contains some of the world's finest examples of early painting from both Italy and Northern Europe, was from the first destined to hang in the new wing. It has been designed with these works specifically in mind, and the arrangement and dimensions of the new galleries have been carefully planned to provide sympathetic spaces in which to view the collection of some 250 paintings.

To hang a sequence of works such as these is a complex task: variations in scale, size and subject are enormous, ranging from small Netherlandish portraits, and tiny devotional pictures, to huge altarpieces. It was therefore necessary for the architect to design rooms of varying size and height; at the same time he rightly wanted the whole floor of galleries to have the consistent ambience of a grand set of public rooms. The number of people coming to visit the Gallery is more than three million annually, and the numbers increase year by year.

Robert Venturi has designed the galleries in three ranges of rooms running north-south the length of the building. The central range is the highest, with hanging walls of 5.5 metres, followed by the eastern range, most of which is 5 metres, and the western range, which has walls of 4.5 metres. The central range provides a nave-like spine to the building, and consists of an enfilade of four rooms linked by broad arched openings, like the Dulwich Picture Gallery. This fine vista is terminated at each end by an altarpiece.

The completion of the Sainsbury Wing has meant a major rehanging of the entire National Gallery Collection. In order to make the increased gallery area comprehensible and manageable, the pictures are to be hung in four chronological groups in different wings of the building. In the Sainsbury Wing the visitor can now see the effects of the Early Renaissance on artists working on both sides of the Alps. Masaccio and the artists of the early Italian Renaissance are shown close to their Netherlandish contemporaries Campin, van Eyck and Rogier van der Weyden; Antonello now hangs near Bouts and Memlinc; and the late fifteenth-century masters, Bellini, Mantegna, Perugino and Raphael close to their Northern contemporaries Gerard David, Massys and Dürer.

Emphasis has been given to certain key works in the Collection by their positioning. *The Wilton Diptych*, Jan van Eyck's *'Arnolfini Marriage'*, Piero della Francesca's *Baptism of Christ*, Cima da Conegliano's *Incredulity of Saint Thomas*,

Raphael's *Crucified Christ*, and Leonardo da Vinci's *Virgin of the Rocks*, now hang in conspicuous locations – often at the end of a long vista where they can be seen and recognised at a distance from neighbouring rooms.

To help the curators plan the 'ideal hang' for the new galleries a scale model (1:20) was made of the gallery floor and scale photographs were taken of every picture. These miniature paintings were hung, moved and juxtaposed in 'the doll's house' for many months until a workable plan was achieved. What the visitor sees today is the product of a lengthy period of experiment and discussion. The arrangement is likely to be fairly permanent because there is little chance that the gallery will acquire many more paintings of this period.

From the top of the grand staircase a view with a diminishing architectural perspective extends across the northernmost galleries to Cima's large *Incredulity of Saint Thomas*, which with its life-size figures, perspectival recession and naturalistic light gives an amazing illusion of life.

Room 51 is the first gallery and it houses both the beginning and the end of the Early Renaissance collection. Giotto meets Leonardo here across a gap of 200 years. With your back to the Leonardo *Virgin of the Rocks* you will see the great altarpiece of *The Coronation of the Virgin* by Jacopo di Cione in the distance on the wall of Room 53. One of the treasures of the Collection, *The Wilton Diptych*, is placed in a case in the centre of Room 53.

Through the doorway from Room 54 can be seen one of the most popular pictures in the National Gallery, Uccello's *Battle of San Romano*, carefully placed so that it can be enjoyed at a distance as well as close up. This picture may have been painted for a Medici palace in Florence and it now hangs in Room 55 with two other Medici paintings, Filippo Lippi's *Seven Saints* and *Annunciation*. The last room of the eastern range, Room 56, has a different architectural character. It is an irregular shape, with oak instead of marble skirtings. This room houses the small early oil paintings by Jan van Eyck, Robert Campin and Rogier van der Weyden.

The four central rooms with their large arched openings house the majority of the Italian paintings of the second half of the fifteenth century and in particular a number of great altarpieces of this period. There are two major vistas in these rooms: one allows a view to the east through to a window on the grand staircase and aligns *The Wilton Diptych* in Room 53 with the roughly contemporaneous Austrian *Trinity* in Room

63; the other vista runs north-south from Raphael's *Crucified Christ* to *The Demidoff Altarpiece* on the south end wall.

In the western range, Rooms 61–6, the largest room is the most northerly, Room 61. Here, as well as the Cima altarpiece that is the climax of the columned east-west axis from the top of the staircase, there are remarkable paintings by Bellini and Mantegna. Late Netherlandish and German paintings hang in Rooms 62 and 63, while in the two linked galleries, Rooms 64 and 65, paintings by Italian and Netherlandish artists working in the middle years of the fifteenth century are juxtaposed.

Room 66 houses the National Gallery's three works by Piero della Francesca, *The Baptism of Christ, Saint Michael*, and the late *Nativity*. This chapel-like room has a stone floor and *The Baptism* is hung in a shallow niche terminating the vista from Room 63.

Off Room 51 is a small space specially designed for the Leonardo Cartoon of *The Virgin and Child with Saint Anne and Saint John the Baptist* – a work on paper which is therefore displayed in reduced light. This work is a fitting preparation, in its psychological complexity and sophistication of composition, for the masterpieces of the sixteenth century which are shown across the circular bridge of the Sainsbury Wing in the old building.

A scale model of the new galleries was made to simplify the process of hanging the pictures. The curators experimented with miniature photographs of the paintings to find the ideal arrangement, and to take best advantage of the architectural vistas of the new wing.

LIGHTING

David Saunders

The lighting design in the Sainsbury Wing uses daylight to the greatest extent possible and in a manner that conserves its unique characteristics – variety and changeability. Most museum lighting systems that employ daylight at all are designed to iron out its variations in order to achieve 'ideal' conditions for viewing and conservation. The result is a hermetic environment divorced from the outside world. The system designed for the Sainsbury Wing allows the light in the galleries to be influenced by the movement of the sun across the sky, a passing cloud or an impending storm. The natural light is supplemented when necessary by artificial lighting, which has been designed to blend sympathetically with fading daylight.

Before the natural and artificial lighting systems were finalised, their applicability was tested using a 1:5 model built on the roof of the National Gallery and a full-scale model at Shepperton Studios. In each case, a portable light-level logging apparatus was positioned in the model to produce a record of light levels and to allow the lighting schemes to be refined.

Two models were built to test the lighting systems for the new galleries, a 1:5 model (above) *and a full-scale model at Shepperton Film Studios* (right).

CONSERVATION CRITERIA

Lighting systems within the Gallery have always been designed to meet internationally accepted conservation recommendations. The recommended maximum illumination for the type of paintings displayed in the new wing is 200 lux. There is no minimum limit imposed by conservation criteria, but studies in museums and galleries have shown that colour and detail are less easily perceived at illumination levels much less than 200 lux. There is in effect a rather narrow band of acceptable levels. In order to allow for natural variation in daylight, and so preserve its principal attraction – that is changeability, the system has been designed to allow a greater degree of short-term variation, while maintaining the same annual exposure of the paintings as would be produced by a fixed level of 200 lux throughout opening hours. The annual maximum exposure has been set, in accordance with recognised practices, at 650,000 lux hours per year. Since the damage suffered by a painting is proportional to total exposure this annual dosage approach is both justified and prudent.

A second potential source of damage to paintings is ultra-violet radiation. This is short-wavelength radiation just outside the range of visible light detectable by the human eye. Ultra-violet is more damaging than visible light to the majority of sensitive materials and colorants. Because of this and the fact that it plays no part in the visual process, ultra-violet radiation is normally removed from both daylight and artificial light in museums and galleries. The generally accepted maximum level for ultra-violet radiation is 75 microwatts per lumen. Natural and artificial lighting in the new wing have been designed to produce less than 10 microwatts per lumen, a significant improvement over common practice.

THE MAIN GALLERIES
Daylight

Daylight is admitted to an 'attic' which comprises a series of chambers located between the galleries. The outer roof is double-glazed, one of the layers being a laminated glass containing an interlayer of a polymeric material which absorbs a high proportion of incident ultra-violet radiation. The passage of light from the outer glazing to the clerestory windows in the lanterns above the galleries is controlled by a bank of motorised louvres. These louvres are positioned directly beneath and follow the contours of the pitched outer glazing. The louvres serve two functions: first to moderate the

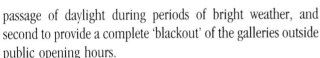

passage of daylight during periods of bright weather, and second to provide a complete 'blackout' of the galleries outside public opening hours.

The clerestory windows, which are present in all but two of the main galleries, are glazed with a diffusing glass decorated with clear vertical borders. The diffusing glass prevents direct sunlight falling upon the lower walls and ensures that visitors are not distracted by the machinery in the roof space, while the border provides a hint of daylight and helps to make the directionality of the natural light apparent.

In four of the galleries at the east of the wing large windows allow some daylight to enter from the grand stair. The glazing in these windows contains an ultra-violet absorbing interlayer. Calculations were made at an early stage of the design to ensure that no direct low-angle winter sunlight would penetrate through these windows into the galleries. Each window is fitted with a translucent blind to allow the level of light to be moderated when the gallery is open and an opaque roller shutter to exclude all light when the galleries are closed to the public. Light levels on the grand stair itself have been reduced by the use of grey-tinted glass in the curtain wall. This prevents visitors in the galleries with windows from being distracted by a bright area to the east of these rooms and assists visitors ascending the grand stair to adjust to the lower light levels of the galleries. The grey-tinted glass used was specially selected to reduce light levels without changing the colour appearance of the exterior scene.

Two of the galleries to the south of the main floor, designed to house smaller paintings, admit daylight through horizontal laylights comprised of diffusing glass panels rather than the lofty lanterns found elsewhere on this floor.

Artificial light

The artificial lighting system in the main galleries is intended to complement and supplement daylight when the latter is insufficient or absent, and to provide light for security and emergency purposes.

The picture lights are low-voltage (12 volt) tungsten-halogen fittings affixed to a track located in a recessed slot around the perimeter of the lantern ceiling and in slots across the centre of the ceiling in the larger rooms. The position of the lights was designed to achieve lighting angles that do not cause a distracting reflected glare from the paintings. In the two rooms with laylights the fittings are located on tracks attached to the laylight glazing bars. To facilitate relamping and re-aiming, the perimeter slots can be accessed from the roof space by way of a hatch.

Tungsten-halogen lamps are more efficient than conventional tungsten lamps and produce light with high colour quality. Unfortunately tungsten-halogen lamps emit quite a high level of ultra-violet radiation. In the new wing all the

Above left *View of the Sainsbury Wing roof showing the 'attic' chambers through which daylight is admitted to the galleries.*
Above *Four of the galleries in the eastern range have large windows that look out onto the grand stair, one of which can be seen in this photograph of the architects' model.*
Below *Light levels on the grand staircase are reduced by the use of grey-tinted glass in the curtain wall.*

lamps are fitted with lenses that have been coated with a material which reduces the ultra-violet content of the light reaching the paintings to well below 10 microwatts per lumen. These pressed-glass lenses also serve to distribute the light uniformly across the wall.

Two sets of picture lights are provided, on separately switched circuits. The first set are fitted with lenses that are pressed from a blue-tinted glass. These lights are switched on throughout opening hours to give an even wash of light across the region of the wall where paintings are hung. The blue glass filter makes the light from the tungsten-halogen lamp appear somewhat cooler and blend rather better with daylight. As daylight contributes only a portion of the light on the paintings, falling rather more on the upper part of the wall, a sense of directionality can be maintained without compromising light levels on the pictures.

The second set of picture lights is fitted with clear glass lenses. These lamps thus provide a warmer light and are only switched on when the combined illumination provided by the combination of daylight and permanent artificial light is insufficient for comfortable viewing. This circuit is activated by internal light sensors as described in more detail in the next section.

One potential problem with fittings of the type used in the new wing is re-aiming the light beam after relamping. This problem is exacerbated in the galleries with clerestories by the long distance between lamp and painting; a slight change in position of the fitting can give rise to a large displacement at the wall. The lights in the new wing are standard commercial fittings that have been redesigned with two locks that allow the aim of the beam to be fixed. It is not necessary to interfere with these locks during routine relamping.

During the winter months daylight fails before gallery closing time. After dark the appearance of the clerestory windows can be unattractive. The solution adopted, and already used successfully elsewhere in the Gallery, is to close the blinds and illuminate the roof space using environmental fluorescent lights located above the lantern glazing. Fluorescent lights are chosen because of their high efficiency and reasonable colour quality. The latter is less important since their contribution to picture lighting is minimal.

Lastly, very efficient high-pressure sodium lamps are used for emergency lighting and to provide sufficient light for security patrols outside public opening hours when daylight is rigorously excluded and all other artificial lights are extinguished. The patrol and emergency lights are directed downwards at the floor and cast very little light on the paintings.

Lighting control

The need to maintain adequate illumination, without exceeding conservation limits while making use of changeable natural light, has led to the development of computerised control systems in the main building. The lighting control installed in the new wing is based upon the experience gained and lessons learned from previous control systems.

In the Sainsbury Wing there is no attempt to respond rapidly to sudden changes in the level of natural light. The level of daylight is constantly monitored by sensors on the roof. Outside public opening hours all the louvres are closed. At the beginning of the day the computer calculates the average level of daylight for the previous fifteen minutes. This value is used to determine whether the blinds should be moved to their seasonal set angle (which will change from near open in winter to near closed in summer), or should be opened fully, if the day is unseasonably dull. This averaging procedure is repeated every two hours to assess changes in daylight level and to respond, if necessary, until the Gallery closes or dusk falls. The long time interval between changes in the angle of the louvres ensures that the visitor beneath is aware of any changes in daylight.

The artificial lights are also controlled by the computer system. During the night all the picture lights are extinguished and the room is lit only by security lights. Before public viewing hours the environmental fluorescent lamps in the roof space are switched on to provide sufficient light for the rooms to be cleaned. When the louvres are opened the security and environmental lights are extinguished and the first set of picture lights, fitted with blue-tinted lenses, are switched on. These remain on throughout the day. In each room six light sensors are located in the recessed slot above the clerestory windows. These constantly monitor the light level on the wall at the height of the paintings, taken to be 1.6 metres above floor level. If the average level of light on the wall over a period of time drops below a set level, the second set of lights are switched on. To avoid a sudden increase the illumination is gradually raised over several seconds until the full output is reached. When the average light level exceeds a second set value these lights are extinguished. The averaging procedure ensures that the lights do not switch on and off in rapid succession in response to periodic small changes in daylight, as might be caused by scattered cloud passing before the sun. The period of averaging and the upper and lower preset values are programmed into the controlling computer and may be refined as necessary.

During a considerable part of the year, particularly in winter, dusk falls before the Gallery closes to the public. The louvres are then closed and the environmental lights in the roof space are switched on. Light from these sources is reflected by the underside of the closed louvres back through the clerestory windows. These lights provide a negligible contribution to picture lighting, but serve to lighten the appearance of the lantern in the absence of natural light. At Gallery closing time all but the security lights are extinguished.

The times of Gallery opening and closing may be adjusted at the controlling computer to account for events such as late night opening or evening functions. To allow the success of the control regime to be assessed, readings from the light sensors are stored by the computer for weekly and annual analysis.

THE LEONARDO CARTOON

Leonardo da Vinci's Cartoon, *The Virgin and Child with Saint Anne and Saint John the Baptist*, is housed in a separate room adjacent to Room 51 on the main floor. Because of the vulnerability of this chalk and charcoal drawing on paper, it is displayed in a showcase glazed with a highly resilient polycarbonate sheet. The fragility of the Cartoon dictates a light level of no more than 50 lux. External light sources are not appropriate since these would be seen reflected in the glazed front of the case. Uniform illumination across the surface of

the Cartoon is provided by light focused from a number of fibre-optic bundles mounted around the perimeter of the case. The tungsten-halogen light source is located well away from the Cartoon to minimize its heating effect while the light-transmitting fibres absorb the ultra-violet radiation emitted by the lamp. Low light levels are maintained in the surrounding room in order to allow the visitor to adapt to the darker viewing conditions and to avoid creating reflections in the glazed front of the case.

TEMPORARY EXHIBITION GALLERIES

The temporary exhibition galleries, which are located below ground level, are perforce illuminated only by artificial lights. The role of these galleries has dictated that the lighting system should be as flexible as possible, so that it may adapt to the installation of new walls or showcases and accommodate the variety of different paintings, drawings and other objects that might be displayed during special exhibitions.

All six of the galleries have a system of lighting track recessed in the ceiling. The number of tracks and distance between them varies with ceiling height to ensure that reflective glare from the paintings and exaggeration of texture by shallow-angle light are avoided.

As in the main floor galleries, low-voltage tungsten-halogen lamps are used in all the picture lights. The light fittings are the same as those of the main floor, except in the rooms with lower ceilings, where a fitting of smaller size has been found to be less obtrusive. Again, all the lights are fitted with pressed-glass lenses to spread the light beam and are specially coated to reduce the ultra-violet content of the light reaching the paintings.

Since the temporary exhibition galleries are used to display works of art that may vary in their sensitivity to deterioration by light, the level of illumination will be set during the installation of the lighting for each new exhibition. Strict conservation requirements, such as a level of less than 50 lux for works on paper or for textiles, are more easily maintained in the absence of daylight.

The control sequence for these galleries is relatively straightforward. Outside opening hours high-pressure sodium security lights illuminate the floor. When the rooms are open to the public the security lights are extinguished and the main picture lights are on. As with the main floor galleries, changes in the opening hours can be programmed into the controlling computer.

CHRONOLOGY

April 1985
The National Gallery accepts the Sainsbury brothers' gift of a new wing

October 1985
Short list of six architects announced:

Henry Nichols Cobb of I. M. Pei Partnership (USA)

Colquhoun and Miller

Jeremy Dixon/BDP

Piers Gough of Campbell, Zogolovitch, Wilkinson and Gough

James Stirling, Michael Wilford and Associates

Venturi, Rauch and Scott Brown (USA)

January 1986
Winning design, by Venturi, Rauch and Scott Brown, selected

March 1987
Final budget approved

April 1987
Public exhibition of the design for the Sainsbury Wing

December 1987
Planning permission granted

January 1988
Construction commences

March 1988
Foundation stone laid by TRH The Prince and Princess of Wales

May 1989
Completion of structure – Topping Out

August 1989
Weathertight

October 1990
Certificate of practical completion

December 1990
Handover to the Trustees of the National Gallery

February 1991
Commissioning of environmental systems complete

April 1991
Picture hanging commences

July 1991
Opening of the Sainsbury Wing by HM The Queen

CONSTRUCTION DETAILS

THE SITE
The Sainsbury Wing is linked to the west end of the National Gallery by a pedestrian bridge spanning Jubilee Walk. The remainder of the site is bounded to the south by Pall Mall, to the west by Whitcomb Street and to the north by St Martin's Street.

CONSTRUCTION
Under the aegis of Sir Robert McAlpine Construction Management Ltd, work on the site began in January 1988. Following the completion of the foundation piling (this included a large-diameter, under-reamed bored pile for each of the internal columns carrying the structure's vertical load), and with the ground-floor slab underway, excavation commenced to a depth of 11 metres in order to accommodate the two basement levels of the new wing. Over 18,000 cubic metres of skilful and meticulous excavation work was carried out, carefully coinciding with the construction of the basement slab; in the final stages the digging and replacement work were alternated to ensure that the underlying clay retained its support to the secant-piled diaphragm walls without drying out.

On 30 March 1988 the foundation stone was laid by TRH The Prince and Princess of Wales, and work commenced on the construction of the reinforced concrete structure. This phase was completed 10 months later and the event was marked by the Topping Out ceremony on 12 May 1989. The 'weathertight' date was met at the end of August 1989 and was swiftly followed by the finishing trades beginning work on the inside of the building. Towards the final stage work continued day and

night. When construction activity reached its peak during March, April and May 1990 there were 22 contracting firms working simultaneously on site, many of whom opted to work double shifts, so that in excess of 300 operatives could be employed at any given time.

The building comprises a reinforced concrete sub- and superstructure sheltered by a complex steel roofing framework. Floors are typically 425-millimetre-thick reinforced concrete slabs, and supporting columns

are aligned on a north-south axis (although not in an east-west direction), at approximately 10-metre intervals. At gallery level there is an 8.5-metre perimeter wall which was cast in one lift, a technique more commonly found in civil engineering. All perimeter walls are vertically cantilevered and this, in conjunction with the structure of the lift shafts and escape-stair walls, provides the stability for the building.

The complex design of the roof structure reflects the various demands imposed by service, maintenance and daylight requirements and these have been solved by a system in which heavy beams support relatively lightweight lattice-type walkway girders set at differing levels. Primary beams run north-south, with central columns bearing on the gallery-level slab. The roofing framework uses 1,800 pieces of structural steel weighing 360 tonnes in total.

EXTERIOR

The external walls, with the exception of the glass wall to the east of the building overlooking Jubilee Walk, are clad variously with Portland stone, Cornish granite and custom-made Ibstock bricks. The front elevation, which faces onto Trafalgar Square and Pall Mall, and the structure of the Jubilee Walk bridge link use a specially selected Portland stone very similar to that which clads Wilkins's building. The Whitcomb Street elevation and the northern façade employ extensive brick cladding. A special mortar made with white Aylett sand was manufactured to complement the light buff rustic bricks and the stonework. The northern aspect of the Sainsbury Wing has relatively plain brickwork, and incorporates a massive stone panel bearing the inscription 'The National Gallery'; a further granite slab is inscribed with a brief history of the Hampton site. Along Whitcomb Street the brickwork is underlined at street level by Portland stone and Cornish granite, which frame the windows of the shop; added to this elevation are also a number of painted, decorative iron columns. The external envelope of the building uses in total 2,400 square metres of Portland stone, 140 square metres of Cornish granite and 115,000 facing bricks with 27

different specials. The interior grand staircase, which rises the full height of the building from the main Trafalgar Square entrance, is screened from Jubilee Walk by a great glass curtain, 300 metres square and made from double-glazed, coated aluminium Parasol glass. After an extensive search suitable glass was located in Belgium and was subsequently manufactured to specification in Holland. From the exterior the grey tint of the glass is

Paintings by Andrew Norris – an artist who recorded the growth and development of the new building at every stage. Concrete pouring (acrylic over linocut), foundation boring, and earth moving (ink and gouache) are shown clockwise.

Above *Ink and gouache painting by Andrew Norris showing the ground floor and a view into the basement in 1988.* Below *A McAlpine group photograph.*

clearly visible, but from the interior there is an unhampered view of the level 5 bridge that links the Sainsbury Wing to the main National Gallery, of the eastern façade of the Wilkins building and of Trafalgar Square. Jubilee Walk and the small garden to the north of the link bridge are paved in a formal pattern with granite and traditional York stone flagstones.

INTERIOR
FLOOR PLANS

The Sainsbury Wing has been designed, in principal, to house the Early Renaissance collection. The 16 main galleries are on the top floor (level 5) – the same level as the main galleries of Wilkins's building, which are aligned on an east-west axis and reached on this level via the bridge link above Jubilee Walk. The new galleries form a series of linked rooms, carefully detailed and planned to suit the character of the collection and to provide the best quality of natural top lighting. To complement the paintings on display the galleries have been designed with a set of Italian Renaissance rooms in mind, the architects' imaginative interpretation of which is revealed in the thoroughly modern idiom that now confronts the visitor.

Other public facilities include temporary exhibition galleries, a cinema and a lecture auditorium in the basement and on the lower ground floor (levels 1 and 2). The ground floor (level 3) houses a large entrance hall, cloakrooms, an information desk and a shop (which has a second entrance in Whitcomb Street). There is a fully computerised information room on the first floor (level 4), as well as a restaurant and coffee bar. The service areas are all located to the north of the building and include loading bays on the ground floor. Also at this end of the building are new storage and packing rooms and additional staff rooms. The basement area is connected to the main building by a link on level 2.

THE GRAND STAIRCASE

The grand staircase, which extends from the Trafalgar Square entrance to the main gallery floor on level 5, occupies the entire eastern length of the Sainsbury Wing. There are 51 steps, which comprise a total distance – including landings – of 35 metres. At its highest point the floor-to-ceiling height is 15 metres. The staircase widens from a 4.3-metre width at entrance level to a full 7 metres by the time it reaches the main gallery floor, which creates the illusion that the staircase is foreshortened when viewed from the bottom and lengthened when looking down from the top.

INTERNAL STONEWORK

Stone has been used for the floorings in all the major circulation areas and provides an extremely hard-wearing finish. Many of the interior walls are also stone clad. The search for suitable materials was extensive and rigorous: stone quarried in England, France, Italy and America was used in the construction of the building and had first to be subjected to an exhaustive testing of finishes. A team of highly skilled stonefixers from Portugal tackled the exacting task of installation, which took over six months to complete.

Limestone

The stone used for internal wall cladding is a French limestone known as Chamesson, chosen for its uniformity of colour and minimal shell content. Quarried in Sogepierre, Chamesson, France, it was manufactured to specification near the quarry and has been employed in the new wing in both a smooth and a rusticated finish.

Granite

The treads of the main staircase are cut from blocks of charcoal-black granite

an Italian sandstone similar to marble. This stone has often been employed in the interiors of Italian Renaissance palaces, and in churches such as the Pazzi Chapel in Florence, designed by Brunelleschi. At the top of the grand staircase there is a series of massive pietra serena columns ranged along the east-west, or 'perspective', axis. In the main galleries all the door frames are constructed of this matt-surfaced stone, together with the skirtings and the margins which surround the floors of all the galleries.

supplied from Cold Spring, Minnesota, USA, and manufactured in Germany where the solid tread and riser units were cut. The tread surfaces have been sandblasted and jetted with high-pressure water to provide a non-slip finish while enhancing the natural sparkle of the stone. The individual

stones are fixed by dowels to the sloping upper surface of the concrete structure of the staircase.

Pietra Serena

After much research and a thorough investigation of working quarries it was decided to use a dark grey pietra serena,

Slate

Slate provides an exceptionally durable surface, particularly in areas of heavy traffic, and it has been used extensively for flooring and skirting in the public circulation areas. The silver-grey slate from Brandy Cragg was supplied and manufactured by Burlington Slate in the English Lake District. The stone is seen to provide a sympathetic complement to the other internal stone finishes of the building.

FLOORS

The main flooring in the gallery areas uses American white oak board, quarter sawn and ammonia fumed. The boards were manufactured in Kentucky, USA, and rigorous selection to ensure uniformity of colour took place, before and after ammonia fuming at the installers' factory in Canterbury, Kent.

ACOUSTICS

In the galleries, Micropor acoustic panels, supplied from Germany, serve to absorb the sound created by the reverberation of visitors' footfalls. The acoustic boards have been incorporated into the fibrous plaster cornice and

Above *Michael Harvey carving the inscription of artists' names in Chamesson limestone above the grand staircase.*
Below right *Stonemason working on the external cornice.*

coving of the lower ceiling structure and are distributed at precise intervals. The upper ceilings of the main galleries are composed of metal acoustic tiles, as used throughout the building – above the grand staircase, where the design of the ceiling is determined by the false perspective, over 400 individually shaped and cut tiles have been employed.

AIR CONDITIONING
Ventilation supply and extract points are housed within the fibrous plaster moulding of the gallery ceilings. A range of interlaced computer programmes have been designed to control the Building Management System, an installation which automatically measures and responds to the varied temperature, humidity and ventilation needs of the galleries. Fire and smoke alarms are also operated by the Building Management System. Taking into account the delicate environmental conditions required to preserve the Early Renaissance collection (which includes paintings on wood panels as well as on canvas), the VAV (variable air volume) boxes, which determine the galleries' quantity and

quality of air supply, ensure that a constant temperature of 21°C and a relative humidity of 55 per cent are maintained.

LIGHTING
A full description of the gallery lighting system can be found on page 128.

INSCRIPTION CARVING
Michael Harvey, assisted by Annet Stirling and Brenda Berman, has been responsible for the design and carving of the stone inscriptions. The letter forms are based on early nineteenth-century typographic examples that would have been in use at the time of the building of the main National Gallery, although the typographic spacing and the shallow relief of the cutting gives the inscription a contemporary twentieth-century appearance. Inside the Sainsbury Wing the inscriptions have been lightly cut into the Chamesson limestone, which provides a fairly soft working surface. The edges of the letters are sharply incised but their internal area has been left with a rough surface which catches and retains the light. On the grand staircase the list of artists' names forms a 25-metre-long decorative frieze (each letter is 50 centimetres high) that gives scale to the vast walls.

FURNITURE
Martin Grierson was chosen from a short list of candidates and commissioned to design furniture for the public areas of the new wing that would specifically complement the architecture. His benches, seats and warders' chairs are all made of English oak and reflect the geometry of the building itself.

1986
The Hon. Jacob Rothschild, *Chairman*
Robert Alexander QC
Sir John Baring
Michael Cowdy
Lord Dufferin
St John Gore
Sir Nicholas Henderson
Caryl Hubbard
Sir Rex Richards
Bridget Riley
Michael Sacher, *died July 1986*
HRH The Prince of Wales
Stuart Young, *died August 1986*

1987
The Hon. Jacob Rothschild, *Chairman*
Robert Alexander QC
Sir John Baring
Michael Cowdy

Lord Dufferin
St John Gore
Sir Nicholas Henderson
Caryl Hubbard
Sir Rex Richards
Bridget Riley
HRH The Prince of Wales

1988
The Hon. Jacob Rothschild, *Chairman*
Lady Airlie
Lord Alexander QC
Michael Andrews
Sir John Baring
Michael Cowdy
Lord Dufferin, *died May 1988*
Bamber Gascoigne
St John Gore
Sir Nicholas Henderson
Caryl Hubbard
Bridget Riley
Sir Rex Richards
Peter Troughton
HRH The Prince of Wales

1989
The Hon. Jacob Rothschild, *Chairman*
Lady Airlie
Lord Alexander QC
Michael Andrews, *resigned October 1989*
Nicholas Baring
Michael Cowdy
Bamber Gascoigne
St John Gore
Sir Nicholas Henderson, *resigned June 1989*
Caryl Hubbard
Sir Derek Oulton
Sir Rex Richards
Peter Troughton
HRH The Prince of Wales

1990–91
Lord Rothschild, *Chairman*
Lady Airlie
Lord Alexander QC
Nicholas Baring
Michael Cowdy, *resigned July 1990*
Bamber Gascoigne
St John Gore
Caryl Hubbard
Sir Derek Oulton
Sir Rex Richards
Peter Troughton
Euan Uglow
HRH The Prince of Wales

Left *The carpentry team on the main vista of the gallery floor.*
Bottom *View into the roof space showing part of the endless ducting which is now hidden behind the gallery ceilings.*

137

THE PROJECT TEAM

Tom Purdy David Singer

Nancy Rogo Trainer Rich Stokes

George Ross Maurice Weintraub

Mark Schlenker Mark Wieand

Garreth Schuh

ASSOCIATED UK ARCHITECT
Sheppard Robson

William Mullins Elizabeth Aston

Sinclair Webster Andrew Brown

John Hunter Simeon Peerutin

STRUCTURAL ENGINEERS AND SERVICE ENGINEERS
Ove Arup and Partners with Jaros, Baum and Bolles

Richard Haryott Phil Stockman

David Brunt Bill Horn

Iain Lyall Len Harris

Alan Pepper Francis Walley

Sean Ascough Nick O'Riordan

Carl Moses Michael Long

Doug Moulton Jeremy Love

Jonathan Phillips John Nash

Chris Taylor Ian Fowler

Robert Stewart Richard Cowall

Brian Sherriff Richard Bussell

David Hardcastle Margaret Law

Richard Curran Tony Clowes

Ian Feltham Roy Ayres

David Hadden Paul Kelly

Andrew Sikko Brent Coward

Brian Freeth Gareth Young

Barrie Gould Steve Cary

John McDonald Ross McNeill

CONSTRUCTION COST CONSULTANT
Gardiner and Theobald

Michael Coates Maurice Oldfield

Peter Coxall Peter Wilford

SERVICES COST CONSULTANT
Mott, Green and Wall

Derek Mott Nick Mulholland

Barry Nugent Peter Gallot

SPECIAL CONSULTANTS
Acoustics
Arup Acoustics

Audio-visual
Technical Planning International

Glazing Systems
Cladtech Associates

Landscape Architect
Armstrong Bell Landscape Design

Lighting
Jules Fisher and Paul Marantz, Inc.

ADVISERS TO PROJECT MANAGER
Contract Law Documentation
McKenna and Co.

Company Secretary and Company Law
Denton Hall Burgin and Warrens

Accounting Services and Financial Advice
Clark Whitehill

Insurance
Heath Fielding Insurance Broking Ltd

Planning Approvals
Montagu Evans

Freight and Customs
Wingate Johnston

SPECIAL COMMISSIONS
Inscription Lettering
Michael Harvey
Assisted by Annet Stirling and Brenda Berman of Incisive Letterwork

Gallery Furniture
Martin Grierson

Restaurant Paintings
Paula Rego

TRADE CONTRACTORS
(*In order of appointment*)

Preliminary Works
L. and B. Haulage Ltd

Bored and Secant Piling
Bachy Bauer Consortium

Street Level Slab
Dormers Builders (London) Ltd

Concrete Structure
Diespeker Concrete Co. Ltd

Structural Steelwork
Booth Steelwork Ltd

Spray Fire Protection
Morceau Aaronite Ltd

Roof Membranes and Finishes
Asphaltic Contracts Ltd

King James II surveys the classical growth of the National Gallery.

Wilkins's building and Nelson's Column reflected in the glass curtain wall of the new grand staircase.

Rooflights
Grill and Grossmann GmbH

Brickwork and Blockwork
Irvine Whitlock Ltd

External Stonework
Easton Masonry Co. (Portland) Ltd

Composite Windows and External Doors
Josef Gartner and Co. (UK) Ltd

Services
Crown House Engineering Ltd

Environmental Control System
Satchwell Control Systems Ltd

Fire Alarms and Security Equipment
Racal-Chubb Security Systems Ltd

Commissioning
Commissioning Management Ltd

Lifts
Fujitec (UK) Ltd

Catering Equipment
Catering Consultants and Planners Ltd

Internal Stone
Bonnel Natursteine GmbH

Internal Partitions and Plasterwork
Jonathan James Ltd

Floor Screeds and Granolithic Work
Avondale Construction Ltd

Wall and Floor Tiling
W. B. Simpson and Sons Ltd

Joinery
Russell Brothers (Paddington) Ltd

Hollow Metal Doors and Frames
Jandor Metal Doors Ltd

Hardwood Flooring
Colin Cheeseman Joinery Ltd

Suspended Ceilings
Thermofelt (Contracts) Ltd

Architectural Metalwork
A. Edmonds and Co. Ltd

Ornamental Ironwork
Cromwell Ironmasters (St Ives) Ltd

Utility Metalwork
Cromwell of Reading Ltd

Fire and Security Shutters
Acmex Doors Ltd

Plantroom Flooring
Mortlake Steel Co. Ltd

Scissor Lifts
Britannia Lift Ltd

Electric Coat Conveyors
Bellow Machine Co. Ltd

Miscellaneous Steelwork
J. S. Edwards Ltd

Loading Bay Doors
Crawford Door Ltd

Floor Coverings
Tyndale Carpets Ltd

Roof Blinds
Technical Blinds Ltd

Lecture Theatre Seating
Installed Seating Ltd

Decorations
Smith Decorators of Newbury Ltd

External Civil Works
Online Construction Ltd

External Masonry
Tudor (Architectural Masons) Ltd

Landscaping
Willerby Landscapes

Audio-visual Installation
Sarner UK Ltd

SITE SERVICE CONTRACTORS
Scaffolding
Anglewest Ltd

Site Attendance
Wall Bros. Ltd

Site Security Alarm System
Ace Security and Electrical Ltd

Site Security
Imperial Ltd

SELECT
BIBLIOGRAPHY

HISTORY OF THE NATIONAL GALLERY
AND THE HAMPTON SITE
'An Assessment of the Entries for the National
Gallery Competition', *Architects' Journal*,
27 August 1959, pp. 86–95.
'Design for the Proposed National Gallery', *The
Builder*, 25 May 1867, p. 367.
'The Designs for the new National Gallery', *The
Builder*, 12 January 1867, pp. 23–4; 19 January
1867, pp. 40–2; 26 January 1867, pp. 56–8;
2 February 1867, pp. 70–3; 9 February 1867,
pp. 92–3.
'Extension to the National Gallery', *The
Builder*, 21 August 1959, p. 47.
'Facade of the National Gallery', *The Builder*,
24 October 1891, p. 312.
Grubert, H., *The 1866 Competition for a New
National Gallery*, MA Thesis, Courtauld
Institute of Art, London, 1967.
Harling, Robert, 'The National Gallery
Controversy: Sir Albert Richardson looks at *The
Sunday Times* prizewinners and makes his own
choice', *The Sunday Times*, 14 June 1959,
pp. 27–8.
Harling, Robert, 'Youth States its View', *The
Sunday Times*, 21 June 1959, p. 13.
History of The King's Works; Volume V, edited
by H. M. Colvin, HMSO, London, 1976; Volume
VI, edited by H. M. Colvin, HMSO, London, 1973.
'The Improvements near Charing Cross',
Gentleman's Magazine, London, March 1831.
Liscombe, R. W., *William Wilkins 1778–1839*,
Cambridge University Press, London, 1980.
Martin, Gregory, 'Wilkins and the National
Gallery', *Burlington Magazine*, cxiii, London,
1971, pp. 318–29.
Mullaly, Terence, 'Expanding the National
Gallery', *Daily Telegraph*, 2 July 1958.
'The National Gallery', *The Athenaeum*, 31 May
1834, p. 408.
'The National Gallery', *The Builder*, 19 January
1867, p. 50.
The National Gallery 1938–1954, The
National Gallery, London, 1955.
'The National Gallery. Arrangement of Picture
Galleries Generally', *The Builder*, 14 June 1845,
pp. 282–4.
'The National Gallery Competition: Winners of
the £5000 prizes', *The Sunday Times*, 7 June
1959, pp. 22–3.
'The New Courts of Law and the National
Gallery Competitions', *The Builder*, 10 March
1866, p. 177.
'The New National Gallery', *The Builder*,
21 August 1852, p. 528; 12 September 1857,
pp. 522–3.
'The New National Gallery', *Return to an

*Order of the Honourable House of Commons
for Copies of the Correspondence between Her
Majesty's Office of Works and the Architect of
the New National Gallery*, 23 May 1870.
'New National Gallery Designs', *The Builder*,
16 March 1867, p. 180.
'On the Change in the Line of Front of the
Buildings for the National Gallery', *The
Athenaeum*, 16 February 1833, pp. 104–6.
'Propriety on a Plinth', *Architects' Journal*,
8 July 1970, pp. 54–6.
Reports of the Trustees of the National Gallery,
January 1955–June 1956; July 1956–June 1958;
July 1958–December 1959; July 1962–
December 1964; January 1973–June 1975;
January 1980–December 1981; January 1985–
December 1987.
'A Sense of Occasion', *The Sunday Times*,
7 June 1959.
Summerson, Sir John, *Georgian London*,
Barrie and Jenkins, London, 1962 (1988
reprint).
Survey of London, Volume XX, LCC, London,
1940.
Taunton, Geoffrey, 'The Refurbishment of E. M.
Barry's Rooms', *Journal of Museum
Management and Curatorship*, Number 6,
Butterworth, London, 1987.
Tyack, Geoffrey, ' "A Gallery Worthy of the
British People": James Pennethorne's Designs
for the National Gallery, 1845–1867', *Journal
of the Society of Architectural Historians of
Great Britain*, Volume 33, London, 1990.
Wilson, Michael, *The National Gallery,
London*, Charles Letts, London, 1978.

NEW MUSEUM BUILDINGS
Coolidge, John, *Patrons and Architects,
Designing Art Museums in the Twentieth
Century*, Amon Carter Museum, Forth Worth,
Texas, 1989.
Hatje, Gerd, *James Stirling, Die Neue
Staatsgalerie Stuttgart*, Staatsgalerie, Stuttgart,
1984.
Klotz, Heinrich, *New Museum Building in the
Federal Republic of Germany*, Goethe
Institute/Deutsches Architekturmuseum,
Frankfurt A. M., 1985.
Montaner, J. M. and Olivieras, R., *The New
Museums of the Last Generation*, Academy
Editions, London, St Martin's Press, New York,
1986.
Montaner, J. M., *New Museums*, Architecture
Design and Technology Press, London, 1990.
Prown, Jules David, *The Architecture of The
Yale Center for British Art*, Yale University
Press, New Haven, Connecticut, 1977.

Ronner, H., Jhavieri, J. and Dasella, A., *Louis
Kahn, Complete Works 1935–1974*, Yale
University Press, New Haven, Connecticut, 1977.
Searing, Helen, *New American Museums*,
Whitney Museum of American Art/University
of California Press, Berkeley, 1982.
Vergo, Peter, *The New Museology*, Reaktion
Books, London, 1988.

THE WORK OF VENTURI, SCOTT BROWN
AND ASSOCIATES, INC.
The Architecture of Robert Venturi, edited by
Christopher Mead, University of New Mexico
Press, Albuquerque, 1989.
Scott Brown, Denise, *Urban Concepts*, Academy
Editions, London/St Martin's Press, New York,
1990.
Venturi, Robert, *Complexity and Contradiction
in Architecture*, The Museum of Modern Art
Papers on Architecture in association with the
Graham Foundation for Advanced Studies in the
Fine Arts, Chicago, 1966.
*Venturi and Rauch, Architectural Monographs
1*, edited by David Dunster, Academy Editions,
London, 1978.
*Venturi, Rauch and Scott Brown: A
Generation of Architecture*, (exhibition
catalogue), Krannert Art Museum, University
of Illinois at Urbana-Champaign, 1984.
Venturi, Rauch and Scott Brown, edited by
A. Sanmartin, Academy Editions, London, 1986.
Venturi, Robert, Scott Brown, Denise and
Izenour, Steven, *Learning from Las Vegas*,
MIT Press, Boston, 1972.
Venturi, Robert, and Scott Brown, Denise, *A
View from the Campidoglio, Selected Essays
1953–1984*, Icon Editions, Harper and Row,
New York, 1984.

INDEX

Figures in *italic* refer to illustrations

ILLUSTRATION ACKNOWLEDGEMENTS

The publisher has made every effort to trace the owners of the pictures but in some instances details may not have been available.

Cover Photo: Phil Starling.
Title page Venturi, Scott Brown and Associates, Inc.
Back cover Photo: Phil Starling.
Page 19 Interior of 100 Pall Mall by F. MacKenzie, courtesy of the Board of Trustees of the V&A.
Page 21 Royal Mews designed by William Kent, Museum of London; The New Opening to St Martin-in-the-Fields, Mary Evans Picture Library.
Page 22 John Nash's plan of Trafalgar Square, by permission of the British Library, London.
Page 23 Bust of Wilkins, courtesy of the Master and Fellows of Trinity College, Cambridge.
Pages 26–7 Museum of London.
Pages 28 Railton's proposal for Nelson's Column, by permission of the British Library, London; Queen Victoria at the Royal Academy, The Illustrated London News Picture Library, London.
Page 29 Unknown design for the National Gallery, Museum of London; Arthur Allom's design for the National Gallery, Mary Evans Picture Library; daguerrotype of the National Gallery, Trustees of the Science Museum, London.
Page 30 Entrance stairs at the National Gallery, by permission of the British Library, London.
Page 31 Murray's design for the 1866 competition, British Architectural Library, RIBA, London; Street design for the 1866 competition, crown copyright, reproduced with permission of the Controller of HMSO, photo: courtesy of the Board of Trustees of the V&A.
Pages 32–4 The British Architectural Library, RIBA, London.
Page 35 The Illustrated London News Picture Library, London.
Page 37 The Hulton Picture Library.
Page 39 Hamptons, Times Newspapers Limited; design for an extension by Donald McMorran, estate of Donald McMorran.
Pages 40–1 Times Newspapers Limited; extracts of *The Sunday Times* reproduced by

permission of the British Library, London.
Page 44 Ahrends Burton and Koralek, photos: John Donat; Arup Associates Architects + Engineers + Quantity Surveyors, photo: crown copyright, reproduced with permission of the Controller of HMSO.
Page 45 Richard Rogers Partnership, photo: crown copyright, reproduced with permission of the Controller of HMSO.
Page 46 Covell, Matthews, Wheatley Architects, photo: crown copyright, reproduced with permission of the Controller of HMSO.
Page 47 Skidmore, Owings and Merrill; Sheppard Robson; Cullearn and Phillips, photos: crown copyright, reproduced with permission of the Controller of HMSO.
Page 49 Ahrends Burton and Koralek, photo: John Donat.
Page 52 Burrell Collection, photo: David Liddle; Louisiana Museum of Modern Art, Humlebaek.
Page 53 Pompidou Centre, photo: Peter Baistow; Staatsgalerie, Stuttgart.
Page 54 Photo: Richard Bryant/Arcaid.
Page 55 Exterior façade of the Portland Museum of Art (photographed by Brian Vanden Brink); interior façade of the Portland Museum of Art (photographed by Steve Rosenthal); Museum of Fine Arts, Boston, West Wing and Second Level Corridor in West Wing, 18 December 1986, courtesy, Museum of Fine Arts, Boston.
Page 56 Courtesy of The Arthur M. Sackler Museum, Harvard University, Cambridge, Massachusetts, photo: Elizabeth Gombosi; Turner Bay, Fourth Floor Gallery, Yale Center for British Art, New Haven, Connecticut, photo: Richard Caspole; Dallas Museum of Art, Oldenburg, Claes Thure (American, born Sweden 1929), and van Bruggen, Coosje (Dutch, born 1942), *Stake Hitch*, 1984, aluminium, steel, urethane foam . . ., H 53ft 6in × W 15ft 2in × L 44ft 6in, 1984.52.a., Dallas Museum of Art, commissioned to honor John Dabney Murchison, Sr. for his arts and civic leadership, and presented by his Family.
Page 57 Kimbell Art Museum, Fortworth, Texas, photo: Michael Bodycomb; Sainsbury Centre for Visual Arts, University of East Anglia,

housing the Robert and Lisa Sainsbury Collection, photo: James Austin.
Page 58 Photo: © Martin Charles.
Page 59 Henry N. Cobb, Pei Cobb Freed and Partners.
Page 60 Colquhoun Miller and Partners.
Page 61 Jeremy Dixon. BDP.
Page 62 CZWG.
Page 63 James Stirling, Michael Wilford and Associates.
Pages 64–5 Venturi, Scott Brown and Associates, Inc., house in Connecticut (exterior and interior), photo: © Cervin Robinson.
Pages 67–71, Venturi, Scott Brown and Associates, Inc., Gordon Wu Hall, Princeton University (exterior and interior), photo: Tom Bernard.
Pages 72 Sheldonian Theatre, photo: Thomas-Photos, Oxford; St Mary-Le-Strand, The Parish of St Mary-Le-Strand with St Clement Danes; Scala Regia Staircase, Scala Florence.
Page 73 Gallery level floor plan, Venturi, Scott Brown and Associates, Inc.
Pages 74–83 Venturi, Scott Brown and Associates, Inc.
Page 80 A capital, photo: Astrid Athen.
Pages 84–125 Photos: Phil Starling.
Page 127 Times Newspapers Limited.
Page 128 1:5 model, photo: Colin Harvey; Shepperton Studios, photo: David Saunders.
Page 129 View of the Sainsbury Wing roof, photo: Astrid Athen; the architect's model of a gallery, Venturi, Scott Brown and Associates, Inc.; glass wall and staircase, photo: Phil Starling.
Page 130 The louvres, photo: David Saunders.
Page 132 Foundation stone ceremony, Hampton site from New Zealand House, concrete floor slab, photos: Astrid Athen.
Page 134 Photo: Astrid Athen.
Page 135 Portuguese stonemasons, photo: Phil Starling; Italian stone mason, photo: Liz Aston, Sheppard Robson.
Page 136 Michael Harvey, photo: Phil Starling; stone mason working on an external cornice, photo: Astrid Athen.
Pages 137–40 Photos: Phil Starling.